~ A TROPHY OF GRACE ~

The Woman at the Well

Rose Alexander

Ark House Press
arkhousepress.com

© 2025 Rose Alexander

All rights reserved. Apart from any fair dealing for the purpose of study, research, criticism, or review, as permitted under the Copyright Act, no part may be reproduced by any process without written permission.

Scripture quotations marked (NLT) are taken from the Holy Bible, New Living Translation, Copyright © 1996, 2004, 2015 by Tyndale House Foundation. Used by permission of Tyndale House Publishers, Inc., Carol Stream, Illinois 60188. All rights reserved.

Scripture quotations marked (KJV) are taken from The Authorized (King James) Version. Rights in the Authorized Version in the United Kingdom are vested in the Crown. Reproduced by permission of the Crown's patentee, Cambridge University Press.

Scripture quotations marked (NKJV) are taken from the New King James Version Women's Study Bible, 2nd Edition, Copyright 1982 by Thomas Nelson, Inc.

Cataloguing in Publication Data:
Title: The Woman At The Well
ISBN: 978-1-7638801-1-5 (pbk)
Subjects: [BIO005000] BIOGRAPHY & AUTOBIOGRAPHY / Entertainment & Performing Arts; BIO018000   BIOGRAPHY & AUTOBIOGRAPHY / Religious; REL012170   RELIGION / Christian Living / Personal Memoirs;

Design by initiateagency.com

In memory of my parents, Les and Betty, my sister Esther, and my brother Stan.

Acknowledgements

Thank you Liz West for proof reading my manuscript and tidying up spelling.

To Dr Pam Harvey for editing my book and helping me with grammar.

To David Morieson for helping me with the photos.

To Pauline Robins for helping me and giving me your expertise on how to set out my book.

To Ark House for publishing my book.

....

The Woman at the Well

The title for this book came about when I read the story in John's Gospel, Chapter 4, and I realised that this was also my story. Having had many relationships over my adult life in my quest for love, I related to the story of Jesus' encounter with the Samaritan Woman at the Well of Sychar. I could see the similarities with this story as I searched for the Living Water that only Jesus could give.

Contents

Foreword ix
Family Connections xi
Prelude xiii

1	My Childhood	1
2	My Grandparents	8
3	Bimbil	19
4	Working Girl	27
5	Marcus	30
6	Married Life	33
7	Another Baby	38
8	Leaving Home	43
9	Queensland	47
10	Shoalhaven Heads	54
11	Clermont	58
12	Howlong	62
13	My Brother Stan	68
14	Yuendumu N.T.	74
15	Victor James Sophios	79
16	Bible College	85
17	Another Wedding	88
18	Axess Recording Studio	97
19	West'n Rose	100
20	Riverina Girl	104
21	Rose's Family	108
22	Doug's Family	113

23	New Church Update 2022	116
24	My Mum	119
	Mum's Graveside Service-Yeppoon Cemetery	121
	Auntie Margie	125
25	My Friend Ethel	129
26	The Village Redcliffe	133

Conclusions/Tributes/Epilogue 135
Rose's CD's available for purchase 139
Reference List 141

Foreword

By John Orr

My connection with Rose goes back to 1998 when we lived not far from each other – about a ten-minute walk away. Our friendship came about, in one sense by accident, but looking back now, it was all part of God's plan. My wife (Ethel) and Rose met at church, Redcliffe Assembly, now Mueller Community Church.

At the time Rose was married to Vic and a friendship developed between us two couples. Following Vic's passing in 2000, we journeyed with Rose as she mourned the love of her life and her singing partner. Rose sings Country Gospel and for me, that's the best!!

As the friendship grew between Rose & Ethel, it wasn't long before they became partners in the sharing of God's Word. Ethel had been given the gift of the gab!! (In a nice way of course!) And that gift had seen Ethel develop into an accomplished Christian Women's speaker at various functions and conventions between 1977 and 2014.

Between 2001 and 2014 they occasionally accompanied each other – Ethel with her Bible in hand – Rose with her Guitar in hand. They particularly enjoyed ministering to women out in the country and, of course, out in the country, Rose's singing was always appreciated.

There were times when Rose would share her story - and that's where the title of the book comes in. You see, prior to her becoming a Christian – a genuine follower of Jesus Christ – Rose lived a life that, in hindsight, she wasn't proud of. In an endeavor to find peace and happiness, she went from one relationship into another. Never finding satisfaction in any of them. Then she met Christ – and that energy and enthusiasm was redirected to matters that have an eternal perspective.

Over more recent years, as my wife's health has been impacted by Alzheimer's disease, the friendship between Rose and Ethel has not wavered. Rose has faithfully come almost every week to spend time with Ethel or to take her out for coffee together. Something which I have valued dearly.

I warmly commend the story of Rose to you – a lady impacted by the teaching of Jesus to a woman at a well over 2000 years ago.

John Orr, 2025

Family Connections

The Pratt Connection

Charles Pratt married Ann Turner in May 1898 at Wagga Wagga.
Charles Allington Pratt married Martha Swaysland June 1903.
Children: Charles Jnr, Muriel (my Grandmother,) Hilda,
Martha, Esma, Amy, Roy, Roger, Eric, Mabel.
Muriel married John (Jack) Haworth

The Haworth Connection

James married Ruth in England, left England in 1910 for Australia
Children: George, "Jack", (my Grandfather) Edwin, Ruth.
Jack married Olive Muriel Pratt Sept 1924.
Children were Les, (**my Father**) John, James, (Jim) Jean.
Les married Elizabeth Jane Currie "Betty"(**my Mum**) 27 Jun 1946.
Children: Esther Elizabeth, Les Stanley "Stan",
Rose Muriel Dorothy, Leonie Kathleen.
John married Ruth, James "Jim" married Wyn,
Jean married William "Bob" Pritchard.

The Currie Connection

Hugh Currie from Glasgow Scotland married Margaret Kerr from Wales. Children: John Currie from Ayr Scotland married Ann Moir from Kinross England
Children: James Archibald, Goondiwindi Queensland, married Sarah Jane Carson, from Goondiwindi Queensland
Albert James Currie from Goondiwindi married Dorothy Maud Thomas from London, England, married in Hurstville NSW.
(**my Grandparents**)
Children: Tom, Bill, **Elizabeth "Betty"**, Ruth, Margaret.

The Thomas Connection

Thomas Thomas was from Wales married Elizabeth Amelia Goodman from England
Children: Herbert, Elsie, **Dorothy,** Lillian
Dorothy's children: Thomas, William, **Elizabeth**
(**my Mother**), Ruth, Margaret
Elizabeth's children: Esther, Stan, **Rose**, Leonie.

Prelude

As you read my story, you will see the significance of this story to my own life.

Jesus and The Woman at the Well
John Chapter 4 V 4-42

Jesus knew the Pharisees had heard that he was baptizing and making more disciples than John (though Jesus himself didn't baptize them—his disciples did). So he left Judea and returned to Galilee. He had to go through Samaria on the way. Eventually he came to the Samaritan village of Sychar, near the field that Jacob gave to his son Joseph. Jacob's well was there; and Jesus, tired from the long walk, sat wearily beside the well about noon time. Soon a Samaritan woman came to draw water, and Jesus said to her, "Please give me a drink." He was alone at the time because his disciples had gone into the village to buy some food.

The woman was surprised, for Jews refuse to have anything to do with Samaritans. She said to Jesus, "You are a Jew, and I am a Samaritan woman. Why are you asking me for a drink?" Jesus replied, "If you only knew the gift God has for you and who you are speaking to, you would ask me, and I would give you living water." "But sir, you don't have a rope or a bucket," she said, "and this well is very deep. Where would you get this living water? And besides, do you think you're greater than our ancestor Jacob, who gave us this well? How can you offer better water than he and his sons and his animals enjoyed?" Jesus replied, "Anyone who drinks this water will soon become thirsty again, but those who drink the water I give will never be thirsty again. It becomes a fresh, bubbling spring within them, giving them eternal life."

"Please, sir," the woman said, "give me this water! Then I'll never be thirsty again, and I won't have to come here to get water." "Go and get your husband," Jesus told her. "I don't have a husband," the woman replied. Jesus said, "You're right! You don't have a husband- for you have had five husbands, and you aren't even married to the man you're living with now. You certainly spoke the truth!" "Sir," the woman said, "you must be a prophet. So tell me, why is it that you Jews insist that Jerusalem is the only place of worship, while we Samaritans claim it is here at Mount Gerizim, where our ancestors worshiped?"

Jesus replied, "Believe me, dear woman, the time is coming when it will no longer matter whether you worship the Father on this mountain or in Jerusalem. You Samaritans know very little about the one you worship, while we Jews know all about him, for salvation comes through the Jews. But the time is coming—indeed it's here now—when true worshipers will worship the Father in spirit and in truth. The Father is looking for those who will worship him that way. For God is Spirit, so those who worship him must worship in spirit and in truth."

The woman said, "I know the Messiah is coming—the one who is called Christ. When he comes, he will explain everything to us." Then Jesus told her, "I AM the Messiah! Just then his disciples came back. They were shocked to find him talking to a woman, but none of them had the nerve to ask, "What do you want with her?" or "Why are you talking to her?" The woman left her water jar beside the well and ran back to the village, telling everyone, "Come and see a man who told me everything I ever did! Could he possibly be the Messiah?" So the people came streaming from the village to see him.

Many Samaritans from the village believed in Jesus because the woman had said, "He told me everything I ever did!" When they came out to see him, they begged him to stay in their village. So he stayed for two days, long enough for many more to hear his message and believe. Then they said to the woman, "Now we believe, not just because of what you told us, but because we have heard him ourselves. Now we know that he is indeed the Savior of the world." (New Living Translation-NLT).

Chapter 1

My Childhood

Children are a gift from the Lord; they are a reward from Him. Psalm 127:3 (NLT)

I always loved to sing as a teenager. In those days in the 50s and 60s, the latest songs from the radio were written into little books called Songsters. We'd buy them from the record store and my sister Esther and I often went for long walks around the farm, "Bimbil", where we lived outside Griffith, singing our hearts out to the words of the songs in the Songster books. We'd listen to the radio to the latest pop songs and when we finally had a television, we'd watch Bandstand which had all the latest singers on the show. My favourite singer was Little Pattie who had long blonde hair and was a singer from Sydney. She sang surfer girl type songs. I wanted to be like her and as I had blonde hair too and I tried to look like her.

I also loved to sing to the sheep. When they were penned up for shearing, I'd put Mum's lovely black shawl on my head and go down to the shearing shed. I always wanted long hair, so I would wear Mum's lovely black shawl on my head, and I'd walk along the rails and sing to the sheep. They were my audience. I always wanted to learn an instrument as I had a natural ear for music and started writing simple songs when I was on the farm.

I wrote one about Mum and Dad, and one about my brother and sisters, and one about Grandma and Grandad. So I guess my song writing was already there even as a child. I wanted to learn piano, or the guitar, even the bongo drums! Even today, I can often recognise a song on the radio from the 60s and 70s just by the instrumental introduction and can also, more often than not, recognise the singer's voice. I was born Rose Muriel Dorothy at Loretto Private Hospital in Griffith N.S.W. This hospital is no longer there. The doctor that delivered me and my siblings was Dr Solomon Goldberg.

My parents, Les and Elizabeth Jane Haworth lived on a small dry area farm, "Back Micabel" at Tullibigeal, N.S.W. in the central west, not far from Condobolin and West Wyalong. My father also worked away from the farm making dams and channels. He had his pilot's license which he was able to get by correspondence. He flew a couple of small planes in those days. I am the third in a family of four, three girls and one boy. My sister Esther Elizabeth was born in 1947, followed by my brother Les Stanley (Stan) in 1948, then I was born in 1950, then Leonie Kathleen came along in 1952. Leonie was born 4 weeks premature, and she was one of the first babies to be put into a humid-crib which had been invented by a local Griffith man. The three oldest all went to TullibigeaL Public School and we travelled about 50 kms into school in the school bus. I had a several operations in Griffith Hospital when I was about 6, where I had my tonsils removed, all of my baby teeth, and also my appendix. Not all at the same time of course!

Our cousins lived on the farm just over the road. My Mum's sister Ruth was married to my Dad's brother John Haworth. They had 6 children, two deceased, twins Eric and Susan. Susan died at birth and Eric passed away at two and a half during an appendix operation. Then there was Ronnie, Dianne, Jill and Jimmy. We were very close to our cousins and spent a lot of time with them.

We lived at "Back Micabil" until 1956. My grandfather "Jack" Haworth and his brother George had bought the farm and Mum and Dad and the four children lived on the farm there, but Dad was away a lot due to his tank sinking job, which is making dams and channels. I have many happy memories of Tullibigeal even though I was 6 when we left and moved over to Griffith. I went to Tullibigeal Public School and attended Kindergarten and 1st class there. We travelled to school by bus. I can still remember my best friend called Robyn whom I have had contact with recently on social media.

One painful memory was of having my finger shut in the truck door by my brother Stan accidentally, which resulted in a broken finger. Mum took me to the doctor to have it plastered and she told me that the doctor pulled it into place which was excruciatingly painful. That finger still gives me issues now in later life.

Another was of Mum and the four of us coming home from somewhere and the car broke down. It was dark and we had to walk until we came across a neighbors house to get some help. I was always afraid of the dark and it would take many years before I overcame my fear.

There was a terrible flood in the early 1950s and Dad was caught up in them and had to wade through flood waters to get home and as a result he developed pneumonia and was very sick. He was also bitten by a red back spider and almost died.

Loretto Hospital Griffith

The hospital was built in the 1930s by renowned Griffith doctor Solomon Goldberg. Renovations occurred in 2009, blending modern convenience with historic charm which maintained the integrity of the solid, original design.

Solomon Goldberg was certainly one of Griffith's most intriguing historical figures. Born in Palestine in 1901 and graduating with a degree in medicine from Sydney University in 1923, he was contracted by a Griffith medical practitioner which led him to settle in the area. He established the Loretto Hospital on the corner of Hyandra Street and Whitton Street opposite the then Methodist church, and would later return to his home land serving as a medical officer amid Arab and Jewish riots. There he met his wife, Shoshana, and returned to Australia. Dr Goldberg also owned several farms. He purchased a Beelbangera property in the late 1930s which employed a number of Land Army girls as labourers, and another at Benerembah which grew wheat and stock. He also grew opium poppies under licence from the government for the manufacture of medicinal drugs, given the short supply amid the war in Europe. In the mid 1950s Dr Goldberg transported Corriedale sheep from 'Carmel' in Israel, with one group travelling by plane and two shipments by sea. He passed away suddenly in 1966 at the age of 65 while his wife died in 1989. (www.Griffithre.com)

In 1956 we moved over to Griffith. We attended North Griffith Public School which was within walking distance from our house. I repeated 1st class and stayed at that school until we moved once again in 1961 after the death of my Grandfather. My mother had a few jobs and also was a member of the local Griffith Amateur Dramatic Society (called GADS) and we often went to see her perform in a number of plays. I can remember her playing in "The Desert Song", and "Oklahoma", to name a few.

I contacted Glandular Fever during this time and so I spent a number of weeks off school. I wasn't very sporty and would always look for an excuse to have the day off on sports days. I had a number of school friends who I spent a lot of my spare time playing with. We also had lots of cousins to play with as well as my father's Uncle Edwin's children, who had a large family of eleven. There were fun times and I used to love to go out to their farm at Tabbita, just outside of Griffith. We would go rabbiting and had lots of fun with so many cousins to play with. I still have contact with some of those cousins today. Although sadly, one of the boys, Willie, was hit by a car when he was 15 and passed away. At time of writing, Carol, Alwyn and Graeme have all passed away.

I loved ballet and always dreamed of being a ballerina, but with bad knees, this wasn't going to happen. But I did go to ballet lessons for a time and also learned how to tap dance.

There was a boy who lived over the road from us called Alan, and he had a great collection of toy cars. Leonie and I often went over to his place and played in the dirt with his toy cars. His father taught piano and my sister Esther had some piano lessons which she didn't really show any interest in. I would love it to have been me that received those piano lessons. But I had to wait until I left school before I was able to learn to play the piano.

My brother Stan had a couple of mates, Bob and Dennis, and they built a billy cart which they entered into a billy cart race, and won first place. They were fun times living in Barellan St.

I had a number of school friends who lived nearby and we had lots of fun playing together.

Esther, Stan and Rose

Family of 4 - at Tullibigeal

My Childhood

Rose aged 3

Chapter 2

My Grandparents

Proverbs 22:6 says, Train up a child in the way he should go and when he is old, He will not depart from it.

The Currie Connection

My mother's parents, Albert James and Dorothy Maud Currie, lived on a small Soldier Settlers' block at Yenda which is not far out of Griffith. My grandfather, Albert James Currie (known as Bert) had been in the 1st World War and was wounded in the thigh. He was buried alive and only that one of his mates saw his boot move and pulled him out, he would have died. He was awarded a Bravery Medal for this incident. He was on the second shipload that went to Gallipoli, the first shipload didn't make it. He then fought in France. His brother Arthur was killed in the same war. Grandad's mother had passed away when he was just a boy and so he and his brothers and sisters were all farmed out to relatives. Grandad was sent to live with his grandparents and the other five children were all sent to live with relatives. I don't know if I remember meeting his father, Great Grandfather Currie when I was little, or whether I had just seen photos of him as he had lived with

Grandad and Grandma for a time. Grandad's mother was Sarah Jane and after having her first five children, she was advised not to have anymore, but she fell pregnant with her youngest son Arthur and she had birth complications and passed away. The family blamed her husband, my Great Grandfather, and he had a falling out with some. My Grandfather Bert's grandparents were Jewish storekeepers in Inverell in NSW. There is no contact with most of the other siblings as they were sent to different relatives. Grandad's sister Amy was close in age to my Grandfather and I think there was contact with her over the years.

My grandfathers sister Amy, nee Currie, was married to Sydney Clift, a fitter and turner from England. Their daughter Charmian Clift was a very famous Australian author, married to George Johnston, also a well-known Australian author. They wrote many books together.

> Charmian Clift (30 August 1923 – 8 July 1969) was an Australian writer. She was the second wife and literary collaborator of George Johnston.
>
> Clift was born 30 August 1923 in Kiama, a coastal town 120 kilometres south of Sydney. In 1941 she won a Beach Girl competition run by *Pix* magazine and soon after moved to Sydney where she did modelling work to supplement her main job as an usherette at the Minerva Theatre. In 1942, aged 19, she became pregnant and gave up her child for adoption. In April 1943 Clift enlisted in the Australian Army, where she gained the rank of Lance Bombardier in charge of a group of gunners housed in Drummoyne.

Career

After Clift and husband George Johnston's collaboration *High Valley* (1949) won them recognition as writers, they left Australia with their young family, working in London. In November 1954 they relocated to the Greek island of Kalymnos and later Hydra to try living by the pen. She met the songwriter Leonard Cohen while there in 1960.

Johnston returned to Australia to receive the accolades of his Miles Franklin Award-winner *My Brother Jack*. Clift moved back to Sydney with their children in 1964, after which her memoirs *Mermaid Singing* and *Peel Me a Lotus* and her novel *Honour's Mimic* became successes.

She was also well known for the 240 essays she wrote between 1964 and 1969 for *The Sydney Morning Herald* and *The Herald* in Melbourne. They were collected in the books *Images in Aspic* and *The World of Charmian Clift*. In the meantime, Clift and Johnston's marriage was disintegrating under the pressures of their drinking habits and the problems their children had settling into life in Sydney.

On 8 July 1969, the eve of the publication of Johnston's novel *Clean Straw for Nothing*, Clift committed suicide by taking an overdose of barbiturates in Mosman, a Sydney suburb, while considerably affected by alcohol. Academics Paul Genoni and Tanya Dalziell suggest in their 2018 book *Half the Perfect World* that it was the impending publication of Johnston's novel, which Clift knew would lay bare her infidelities while on the island of Hydra, which prompted her to suicide. In her posthumously published article *My Husband George* in that month's edition of *POL* magazine, she wrote:

> I do believe that novelists must be free to write what they like, in any way they liked to write it (and after all who but myself had urged and nagged him into it?, but the stuff of which *Clean Straw for Nothing* is made is largely experience in which I, too, have shared and... have felt differently because I am a different person...

Clift's autobiographical books *Mermaid Singing* and *Peel Me A Lotus* were reissued by Muswell Press in 2021, with new introductions written by novelist Polly Samson, whose own 2020 bestselling novel A Theatre For Dreamers is a fictionalized account of life on Hydra in the 1960s, featuring real-life characters including Clift, Johnston and Cohen.

(Source - www.wikipedia.org)

The Thomas Connection

We spent many happy times out at my Grandparents farm at Yenda, not far from Griffith, and as it was a farm that had irrigation channels to water the crops. My Grandfather would let the water down to water the lawns around the house and my sisters and brother and I would have a wonderful times cooling off in the water. He had also built a park for us with a swing, a seesaw and roundabout. He was such a fun grandfather, despite his war experience. Grandma was born Dorothy Maud Thomas in London and she migrated out to Australia as a young woman with her mother and two sisters, Lilian and Elsie. Her brother, Herbert Thomas came out first with his father, and he was a friend and neighbour of my grandfather.

Grandma's father was Thomas Thomas and he was Welsh. He married Elizabeth Amelia Goodman, who was English, and they had four children. Her brothers were the first to open a wool mill in Wales. After migrating to Australia, Grandfather Thomas worked for Grace Brothers, a big department store in Sydney and he was a buyer of material for the department store. He travelled all over Europe buying fabric and he was a heavy drinker. This resulted in his death in later years from cirrhosis of the liver. That is why my grandmother had a thing against alcohol as it caused a lot of strife when they were growing up. My grandmother eventually married my grandfather and settled at Yenda, living near Uncle Herb's farm. Grandma was related a long way back to one of Queen Victoria's family, but we are not sure who, so whenever she visited her Great Grandmother, she and her sisters had to curtsy to her. Great Grandma lived with Uncle Herb and his wife Hattie after Great Grandfather passed away. Grandad and Grandma had five children, Thomas (Tom), William (Bill), my mother Elizabeth (Betty), Ruth, and Margaret. Bill and his wife Ruth, lived in a small cottage on the farm and Uncle Bill worked for Grandad. My sister Leonie and I had an extended holiday with Uncle Bill and Auntie Ruth when my mother went in to hospital for an operation. They always had a great stock of board games for us to play, many were educational. Uncle Bill and Auntie Ruth then moved over to live at Hillston where he worked on the railway. When he came to Griffith railway with work, he always walked up to see me when I was first married. He was a lovely country man. They had a daughter, Lois, who died at birth and she is buried in the Griffith Cemetary. They were sadly unable to have any more children.

Grandad (Gandy) and Grandma would pick us up every Sunday and we would drive to their church, in the back of Grandad's truck. They belonged to a fairly conservative Brethren Church (Two by Twos, The Way, or the Truth) and had their meetings in my Great-Grandmother's house in Griffith. I believe that the seed was sown back then even though it was years later before I became a Christian. Each Sunday the children were always asked to stand up and say a memory verse for the next Sunday. If we hadn't learned one, we could always say "God is love." My Grandfather was also known as Mr Currie "The Mintie Man" as he always had Minties to give to all the children after the meeting.

The Two by Twos.

Two by Twos (also known as The Truth and The Way) is an international, home-based Christian new religious movement that has its origins in Ireland at the end of the 19th century. The church has no official name; among members, the church is more usually referred to as "The Truth", "Meetings", or "the workers and friends", but when pressed, members deny any official church name. Those outside the church refer to it as "Two by Twos", "The Black Stockings", "No-name Church", "Cooneyites", "Workers and Friends", or "Christians Anonymous". The church's registered names include "Christian Conventions" in the United States, "Assemblies of Christians" "The Testimony of Jesus" in the United Kingdom, "United Christian Conventions" in Australia. These organization names are used only for registration purposes and are not used by members.

The church was founded in 1897 in Ireland by William Irvine, an evangelist with the interdenominational Faith Mission. Irvine soon began independently preaching that the itinerant ministry set forth in Matthew 10 remains the only valid method of evangelism. Church growth was rapid, spreading outside Ireland. Irvine eventually began preaching a new order in which the hierarchy that had developed within the church would have no placement. This teaching became controversial within the church and led to his expulsion by church overseers around 1914. One of the church's most prominent evangelists, Edward Cooney, was expelled a decade after Irvine. The church then became much less visible to outsiders for the next half-century.

Some in the church assert that it is a direct continuation of the 1st-century Christian church. Others in the church believe that a restoration occurred in the late 19th century. Church ministers are itinerant and work in pairs, hence the name "Two by Twos". Members hold regular twice-weekly worship gatherings in local homes on Sunday and midweek. The church also holds annual regional conventions, also for members, and public Gospel meetings. Baptism by immersion as performed by one of the church's workers is required for participation in the partaking of the emblems of bread and wine in the fellowship gathering.

(Source- Two by Two's - www.wikipedia.org)

The Haworth Connection

My father's parents were Olive Muriel Pratt and John "Jack" Harwood Haworth. My Grandfather came out to Australia with his mother Ruth when he was just a boy of seven. He had chest problems from the cold damp English winters. They had tried living in France first, but the climate wasn't right for Jack there either. Jack's father James left England after leaving his eldest son, George to stay and finish his education. James was a grocer by trade and eventually opened his own grocer's store in Canley Vale. George eventually came to Australia at age 13 aboard the ship "The Irishman". (Source "The Blaze on the Grey Box Tree- The Turner Family remembers"). The Pratt's and Haworth's were another branch of the Turner Family.

My Great-Grandfather Haworth died at age 50 from blood poisoning caused by gum disease. My Great-Grandmother Ruth lived to a ripe old age and it was her home where church meetings were held. She was born in England where she met her husband and he was ostracised by his whole family because he had married below his class. There are still a number of his family members in England who will have nothing to do with the Haworths in Australia.

George and his brother John "Jack" Haworth (my grandfather) looked at land around Ungarie in 1923 before deciding to take on a 960 acre block, and called it "Glenlea". The brothers came from the Junee area where they had share farmed for their father- in -law Charles Pratt (the brothers had married sisters)

Another brother of my Grandfather Jack, was Edwin (Ted) and he was born in Australia and he married Mable who was another sister of my Grandmother Muriel. George and Leila and Jack and Muriel travelled with their families by horses and wagons, with all their belongings on board, arriving at "Glenlea" in 1927. There was no house, so on arrival this was the first task. George built a corrugated dwelling and Jack built his home with flat back timber from a nearby sawmill. They lived in tents until the homes were built. The next task was to clear the timbered block and erect fences.

The families endured hardship and poverty with the two families living off the small acreage. Jack obtained a share farming position with the Gavel family on "Back Micabel" in 1932. Jack, Muriel and their sons Les (my father) and John moved to the old house on the property.

After years of struggling during the 1930s and early 1940s with droughts and the depression, Jack decided to move on. He secured a share farming position on a small irrigation block at Griffith and moved there in 1943. Les, my father, and his family stayed on and eventually sold his portion of "Back Micabel" in 1956 and moved to Griffith. (Source- Tullibigeal Centenary 1917-2017 A collection of history and family stories compiled by Janelle Ireland)

John, Dad's brother, and his brothers Jim and Les, my father and sister, Jean grew up on "Back Micabel". They travelled to school by bike and later, horse and sulky to a small bush school. My father was very smart at school and his teacher said that he could go on and have a career in woodwork as he was so good with his hands.

My paternal grandparents were also from the same religion as my maternal grandparents. I remember many happy times at both sets of grandparents' farms as we were growing up.

I remember when my Grandfather passed away and we had to view his body. I hated doing this and had nightmares after it. The same with my Great-Grandmother, after she had died, her coffin was in her home and all of the grandchildren had to walk by and place a flower in her coffin. This really freaked me out!

Great-Grandma had a ladies companion who lived with her for many years. We called her Auntie Elsie, and she always played the organ at the Sunday meetings. She'd had polio as a child and had one leg shorter than the other and had a very high boot so that both her legs were equal. Many years later, she had that leg amputated as it had given her a lot of trouble.

The Pratt Connection

My father's parents were Olive Muriel Pratt and John "Jack" Harwood Haworth. Charles Allington Pratt, my Great Grandfather, took up his first property "Glenfield" about 1900, then in 1914 he purchased a property which was miles east of "Glenfield". Then during 1922 Charles and his wife Martha purchased the homestead block of "Bethungra Park", the area which was then about thirteen hundred acres. At this stage, share farmers were engaged in the wheat growing operations on each of their properties, while Charles managed the sheep and wool growing side of the business.

Two of the share farmers were George and Jack Haworth who eventually married two of Charles and Martha's daughters, Leila and Muriel. In 1927 the "Bethungra Park" property was sold and the family moved to a new home in Balgowlah, Manly. In 1929, the depression set in and the family business interests failed as a result of the down turn. Charles, Martha, and their children Roy, Eric and Mabel moved back to the "Glenfield" property. Charles was in poor health and he suffered a fatal stroke in 1931.

My Great-Grandmother Martha was very musical and relatives and neighbours recall with pleasure the sing-a-longs around the piano at "Bethungra Park". Most of her daughters had piano lessons once a week and that generally coincided with the day the family would stock up on household supplies.

Charles and Martha could play the button accordion, sons Roy and Eric were soon proficient with the instrument. (Source: The Blaze on the Grey Box- The Turner Family Remembers).

I know now where my musical ability came from, as I learned to play piano by ear when I was little, before I had proper lessons when I was sixteen. I wrote a song called "Grandma's Love" which was about both of my grandmothers and the spiritual influence that they had on my life. I recorded it in 2012 on my album, "Riverina Girl".

Four of us going to Church with Grandad and Grandma Currie

Chapter 3

BIMBIL

> *Fathers, do not provoke your children to*
> *anger, but bring them up in the discipline and*
> *instruction of the Lord. (Ephesians 6:4).*

My grandfather (Jack) became very ill in 1961 and he was taken to Griffith hospital with a gall bladder problem and unfortunately, he passed away, at age 59. This was sad time as we all loved my grandfather. He loved for us grandchildren to play with or rub his feet. One of his feet had only 3 toes! My Uncle Jim, my father's brother, and his wife Win and their family lived on the farm at Bimbil in a house a bit further from the main house. After Grandad passed away, they moved over to Wagga Wagga and Uncle Jim worked in an Agricultural company that sold farm implements. Nannie moved into a house in Griffith until her death.

Dad's sister, my Auntie Jean and her husband Bob Pritchard lived not far out of Griffith and eventually in 1969, they moved with their family up to the Atherton Tablelands where Uncle Bob's parents lived. I loved my Auntie Jean as she had the tiniest feet, so when ever I stayed at her place, I'd dress up in her dresses and her shoes. She was the "cool" auntie.

My father then took over his share of the farm and we all moved out to "Bimbil" and made our home there. We travelled to school on the school bus, which we called the "Sardine Can". We had to change schools as the closest school was Griffith Public School on the southern side of Griffith, about 25 kms away and also Griffith High School was next door where we would all eventually attend. My Nannie moved into a house in Griffith and she passed away four years after Grandad from a heart valve complaint, which these days can be easily fixed. I loved my Nannie very much and my memories of her are happy ones when we used to stay with her from time to time. She was a very quiet and shy lady and she often made my sisters and I dresses on her sewing machine. I always used to love to sleep with her in her bed as it always seemed so warm and cosy.

My sister Leonie and I played together often and had cubby houses built in all sorts of obscure places. We loved to play in the big shed which was where the hay was stored to feed the sheep. Also, we played in Dad's blacksmith shop and on the old sulky that was stored there.

A memorable time was when Leonie and I hopped up on Dad's Fordson tractor and started it up, no key needed. Well it took off on us and there was much crying and screaming until Dad hopped up on it and turned it off.

Esther, Stan and I all learned to drive on the farm, as most farm kids do. I learned on a Mini Moke that dad had bought for the farm. I loved to drive down to the mail box and collect the mail. When I went for my drivers license at age 18, I didn't need any lessons! I was over at Tullibigeal staying with my Uncle John and Auntie Ruth when I went for my license at the local Tullibigeal Police Station. The policeman there at the time was called Sergeant "Keg" Cullen. No need to tell you what "Keg" meant! I think he liked a drink or two! Anyway, he took me for a drive around the block, asked me 3 questions from the rule book which I did get right, so, needless to say, I passed!

Every year, Dad would take the family to Sydney for Christmas. We always drove there. Sometimes we'd meet up with our cousins and stay in a share house together, other times we'd stay with family friends, Alf and Dorothy Coyle, who lived at Mona Vale on Sydney's Northern Beaches. Alf and Dorothy became family friends when their son Mike came over from England to work on my Uncle John's farm at Tullibigeal. My Uncle then sponsored his parents and their other two children to come to Australia. They then became life long friends of the Haworth family. Oh what wonderful fun we had. Going to the beach every day. The spray oil man would come along and spray us with coconut oil. No "Slip, Slop, Slap" back then. So, of course, we had many a painful sunburn. This has later come back to bite me as I have had many skin cancers either burnt off or cut out.

A memory that I have about our car trips to Sydney was that we'd stop along the way, Dad would get out of the car and go for a walk somewhere. We'd ask Mum where Dad had gone and she'd tell us that he'd gone to see a man about a dog! I found out years later that he'd stopped to go to the toilet behind a tree!

I have many happy memories of those holidays. Mum bought me my first two piece swimsuit. Esther and I also attended a dance club with Dorothy and we had lots of fun there. It was so refreshing for us country kids to swim and body surf in the waves.

Mum had a medical emergency while we lived at Bimbil. She had adhesions from previous abdominal surgery and the scar tissue had grown in and blocked her bowel. She was seriously ill and had emergency surgery at Griffith Hospital. She almost lost her life, but thankfully, she came through and eventually recovered and returned home. Leonie and I had gone to stay with Nannie Haworth and I'm not sure where Esther and Stan went. Dad had employed a cook to come and cook for us while Mum was recovering. He wasn't a very nice man and we were all glad when he moved on. I remember one day that he went around and put Turpentine on all of the cats bottoms. What a cruel man he was.

I suffered from constipation for a number of years in my childhood. Mum was always trying me on all sorts of concoctions to get me regular. So one day I was in extreme pain so Mum and Dad took me into the Griffith Hospital and they gave me an enema which cleaned me out well and truly!

A favourite entertainment that Leonie and I loved to do was to watch Dad kill a sheep for food. We basically lived on mutton or chicken during our growing up years. He would cut the sheep's throat, then string it up under a tree and let it bleed out, then cut open the front and out would come all of its intestines. Didn't worry us at all! At my Grandfather Currie's place, when he killed a sheep, he'd lay out the intestines, (the bowel) for us kids and he'd give them all names! The bowel was the nine mile, the lungs were the lights, and I can't recall the names for the rest. What fun it was!

Mum had the job of killing the chooks for food. She'd chop off the head and we'd laugh as the chook would make a last ditch effort of running around headless. Mum would then hang it on the clothes line to drain, then our job was to take off the feathers in boiling hot water, then take out the gizzards. I hated that job! It may seem gory to some, but that was farm life for kids in those days.

I loved to read and almost every birthday or Christmas we would each receive a book. No TV in those days. I only ever had two dolls growing up. One was my baby doll Belinda, and the other one was a bride doll. I loved those dolls. We had to make our own fun. I remember as I was reaching adolescence, Mum gave me a book on menstruation and the facts of life. No talking about it, just read this. At high school, the girls would all go in to a darkened room and watch a film on growing up etc, then the boys would have their turn and they would watch a film on boys growing up. I don't know what they were taught. There was no sex education like there is today.

As my sisters and I began our teens, Mum sent Esther and I to a beauty school to learn how to look after our skin and how to wear makeup. I still wear makeup today and moisturise my face twice a day. I don't like going out unless I have my "face on". We were always doing our hair and having to sleep with rollers in our hair at night, which was most uncomfortable. So one year Mum bought us girls a hairdryer for Christmas. Not like the ones today, it was a cap that went over your rollers and had a pipe going in from the motor which blew hot hair in to dry your hair. Like a miniature version of a salon hairdryer. Much better.

We loved our music as I shared with you earlier. So we had many records. Long Play records (LPs) and 45s. The LP's had a whole album of songs, but a 45 only had two songs, one on the A side, usually the hit song of the day, and the B side which you turned over to play, a song not as well known, but often very good just the same. We had a great collection of records and Mum even had many of her favourites from some of the plays she had been in. One of my favourite records was the Nutcracker Suite as I loved ballet, and Winifred Attwell and Jimmy Shand.

A family tragedy

Then a tragedy occurred on the farm (I think it was about 1963), which was to have a devastating effect on our family, especially for my 15 year old brother Stan. My parents were away for the day so my Nannie was staying with us at the farm to look after us. I was home from school due to sickness. My brother was also home that day and so he drove my Nannie's car to the bus stop to pick up my sister Leonie. It was a common practice for farm kids to drive their parents' cars, even out on the road. As my brother drove toward the bus, he saw the children walk across the road and he kept on driving as he thought they had all crossed over. But alas, there was one more little girl to cross the road and she ran out from in front of the bus just as my brother drove by and he hit her with the car. She died instantly. She was only 10 years old. This rocked our family and the little girl's family to the core. My brother was devastated. He ran all the way home and I can still see the look on his face when he ran in to the kitchen and said, "I've just killed a little girl". This little girl was a girl that he often sat with on the bus as they got on so well together. Her name was Marilyn Gibbs, known as Marley and they lived on a farm over the road from us.

My brother left school after that and at the court case it was deemed to be an accidental death and my Nannie was charged with allowing an unlicensed driver to drive her car. My brother began to work on the farm with my father. This was not ideal as my father and my brother never got along together and my father had a pretty short temper. There were many tense moments and I think my father was disappointed in my brother because he didn't have the same desire to become a farmer. He was later to work in a mine at Western Australia, then he became an inter- state truck driver.

There were a number of bad memories of my time out at "Bimbil". I suffered very badly from aching legs in my early teens and spent many a night crying myself to sleep from the pain. Mum took me to the doctor several times but the doctor always said that it was just growing pains. I was to find out many years later at age 30, when my right knee locked one day, that I had suffered from a condition usually only found in adolescence. This condition is called Osteo Condritis Dissicans, a condition like arthritis that destroys the bone cartilage. I was to eventually have two complete knee replacements in my sixties due to the damage to my knee joints.

My father was a very heavy drinker and would often go in to town and come home pretty drunk. Or he would just sit and drink wine until he was argumentative and very drunk. Dad was a very quiet and shy man and I suspect that by drinking, he would come out of himself somewhat. He never really said much to us kids when he had been drinking but he usually gave my mother a hard time. He never really had time for us at all, just to reprimand us if we'd misbehaved. We knew when we were in trouble if we were called in to Dad's office! He would put Mum down and say nasty things to her but I never ever saw him hit her. He seemed to favour my sister Leonie when he'd been drinking and used to get her to sit on his knee. He called her "Balderpuss" which she hated. This came about because when Leonie and I were little and living at Tullibigeal, she and I got into the sump oil in Dad's shed and put it through our hair, so we had to have our hair cut or shaved off to get it out. Leonie's was completely shaved of so that's why he gave her the nick name, "Balderpuss"!

After some years of my father's obnoxious drinking, my mother had had enough of him after he had been on a bender with one of the farm hands for over a week. So she packed us up and drove into my grandmother's house in Griffith. I don't know what really happened but after that my mother and father both started going back to their church and Dad eventually gave up drinking. The farm was eventually sold and Mum and Dad moved into my Nannie's house as she had passed away by then.

They then moved to another farm after we had all married and moved away from home before eventually moving to Wallacia, near Penrith in Sydney where Dad worked for the University of Sydney on their experimental farm. Dad was very unloving and never showed us any affection whatsoever. This was to have an affect on me for many years to come as I craved affection and just wanted to be loved. Many years later, after becoming a Christian, I had some counselling and was able to forgive Dad for his unloving and distant treatment to me. The four of us were afraid of him and it took me until I turned 40 to actually stand up to him. He particularly gave my brother Stan a hard time. In Later years, I had a good relationship with him and I was reminded of this verse from Mark 11 verse 25 which says: *And whenever you stand praying, forgive, if you have anything against anyone; so that your Father also who is in heaven may forgive you your transgressions.*

Grandad Haworth

Nannie Haworth

Chapter 4

Working Girl

> *Don't be afraid, for I am with you. Don't be discouraged, for I am your God. I will strengthen you. I will hold you up with my victorious right hand. Isaiah 41:10 (NLT)*

After leaving school in 1965, I found a job at G.J. Coles in Griffith as a sales girl and worked there for 4 years. I enjoyed working with people and I was stationed on the men's wear and hardware counter in the days when it was personal service. I worked with an Italian girl Marisa, she taught me how to count in Italian, which I can still do, and she also taught me a couple of swear words! I still see her from time to time when I go back to Griffith.

As a teenager I was very popular with boys. I had a number of boyfriends before meeting a boy who was an Italian, and he played the drums in a band. I was sixteen at the time and even though I liked him a lot I didn't want to just be with the one boy, so I broke it off with him. I think he was disappointed and hurt and I have often regretted my decision.

I was always attracted to musicians and so my next boyfriend was also a musician and he played guitar in a band. He was also an Italian and I found out later that his parents had a nice Italian girl picked out for him. I was very hurt and felt that I had been used. I eventually recovered from this, my first heartbreak experience and I moved on. I went out with several other boys but nothing serious and was enjoying my life. I had several best friends and we often went out to the local dances together. I loved to dance and I especially enjoyed the live bands.

Every Friday night at the local Police Boys Club, there would be a dance with some great local bands in the 1960s to 1970s and my favourite band was The Glentones. Peter Smith was the lead singer and had a remarkable voice very much like Roy Orbison. My sister Esther and I went to the dance every Friday night. This is where most of us met our future partners. In those days, the dances were the quickstep, the waltz, etc. Most of us learned dancing at school, until the twist and the stomp came out, then you didn't even need a partner!

There was also a local hall called the Woodside Hall at the Griffith Showgrounds which held dances, and a number of well known pop stars came to perform. I remember seeing The Bee Gees in their early years, and Normie Rowe to mention a few. Then the dances shifted to the Yoogali Club which was just out of Griffith, and the bands played there instead. This was a licensed club so alcohol was sold there.

I was always very musical and had an ear for music. I had always wanted to learn a musical instrument so my friend Marie and I, at age sixteen, started piano lessons with an elderly lady, Mrs Whiting. I was taught the chord method which was an easy way of playing piano. I had two years and really loved the piano. My Nannie had left her piano in the house where she had lived, so I practiced on that. I eventually bought myself a lovely new piano on hire purchase. This was unfortunately repossessed after I was married.

I remember when we were to have a piano recital for our parents and I was so anxious about playing in front of anyone else, that I had a severe back ache that was so bad, Mum had to call the doctor. They did house calls in those days. This happened again the second year that we had to do a piano recitals and I realise now that it was an anxiety or panic attack. It took me a few years before I was able to sing or play in front of an audience. Marie and I remained friends for several years and eventually lost contact with each other. I have since met up with her again as we've became friends on social media.

I had lots of lovely girl friends and some of them I'd lost touch with over the years, but through the wonders of social media, I've reconnected with. That has been special.

Chapter 5

Marcus

> *I will be glad and rejoice in Your unfailing love,*
> *for You have seen my troubles, and You care about*
> *the anguish of my soul. Psalm 37:7 (NLT)*

Unfortunately, my next romantic entanglement was to cause me much grief for the rest of my life, in some ways. I was 18 when I met Marcus, and my sister's boyfriend had organized a double date with him and my sister and so began a relationship that should never have been.

Marcus came from a dysfunctional family and his father was an alcoholic and very violent man. He was very cruel to his two sons, often killing their pets or burning their toys. Marcus had a brother Philip, who was my age and we had actually been to school together. Marcus' father Eric was a shearer and he was often away from home for several months at a time. He had some Aboriginal blood in him as his mother was a quarter cast Aboriginal and she married an English man. I don't know anything else about his family origins.

His mother Gladys, worked at the local Griffith Hospital as a cleaner and worked there for many years. I had a good relationship with Gladys and she seemed happy with our relationship. Gladys and Eric were separated but lived in the same house when he came home from his shearing trips. Gladys had a special friend, and she slept over in his caravan at the back of the local hotel at night and then came home early in the morning and then went off to work. This had gone on for quite a number of years and apparently many people knew about it and then Marcus' father eventually told me about it. Marcus never mentioned it to me at all and never talked about it.

Gladys had been married previously and she had four daughters. I don't know the real story but all I know is that when the marriage broke up, she was estranged from her four daughters and she never saw them for many years. She did meet up again with a couple of them in later years.

Philip was killed in 1973 after being kicked in the stomach by a policeman up at Darwin in the Police Station. He had been working on the prawn trawlers and he and a couple of his mates were out on the town and were picked up by police for being drunk and disorderly. They were put into the lockup for the night and whatever happened, no-one is sure. A very heavy policeman kicked him in the stomach and perforated his bowel. He was eventually taken to hospital where he developed peritonitis and pneumonia and was put on a plane to be flown to Brisbane but he passed away on the way. His mother had flown up to be with him and she was with him when he died. Eventually there was court case which resulted in an open verdict. The policeman was then moved on.

As our relationship developed I decided to tell Marcus that I had been going steady with an Italian boy. Marcus had a real racist attitude to Italians. The night I told him he went crazy in the car and nearly rolled it over. He broke it off with me and we didn't see each other for a couple of months. Then we reconciled and started going steady. We were eventually intimate which resulted in my falling pregnant. I just wanted to leave home and get away from Dad. We were engaged by then as he had asked me to marry him. When I told

Marcus that I was pregnant he never said that he didn't want to marry me. We had to face my parents and my father was not very happy at all.

I had a falling out with my best friend Marie who came to tell me that Marcus was seeing another girl behind my back. She told Marcus she was going to tell me. He said, "I don't care, you can tell her, but I know who she'll believe!" So, of course, I naively believed him and I didn't even ask my friend to the wedding. Looking back, it was a shame, as she was my best friend.

Mum and Dad then organized our wedding very quickly and we were never asked what we wanted to do. In those days, you either had to get married or you went away to have the baby and it was then put up for adoption. I am so glad that I didn't have that experience and that Marcus and I married on the 21st November 1969. I was only 19 and he was 21. We were married in the Presbyterian Church and had the reception at home. Mum put on a nice salad and we just had a few friends and my family. We had an argument at the wedding but I can't remember what it was about. Marcus always used to make comments about other women and what he would like to do to them. We went to Albury for our weekend honeymoon and it wasn't a very pleasant time. Marcus pouted all weekend and I suppose he regretted our hasty wedding. We then found a small flat to rent and so began our married life.

Chapter 6

Married Life

*The Lord is a shelter for the oppressed, a refuge
in times of trouble. Psalm 9:9 (NLT)*

I had severe evening sickness with my pregnancy and so was unable to go out on Saturday nights like we used to. But this did not stop Marcus from going out anyway. He often went out without me. I remember receiving an anonymous letter from someone warning me that Marcus was seeing another woman. When I confronted him with it, of course, he denied it. Then when I went into hospital to have my son, some other woman came and told me that Marcus was playing up with some girl. This was to go on throughout the rest of our marriage.

I gave birth to Jamie Mark on the 11th June, 1970. Jamie weighed 7lb 2 ½ ozs. He was a lovely little baby with very fair hair. There were many nights that I went to bed crying with my little boy, after Marcus came home from the club or pub after drinking, and abuse me. This was to be a common occurrence for the duration of our marriage. His favourite abuse was to put his hands around my neck and try to choke me. I was often left with red marks and broken blood vessels around my neck. Now it is an offense to try to choke a woman like that. I had several black eyes from his abuse. The abuse that really hurt me was his verbal abuse. He would say some very nasty things to me when he'd been drinking. The saying, "Sticks and stones will break my bones, but names will never hurt me" is a fallacy!

Marcus was always a very snappy dresser. He once bought a white suit and teamed it with a dark blue shirt and tie, this really impressed the ladies! He had a moustache and mutton chop sideburns which were popular in the 1970's. He liked to draw attention to himself and being tall, dark and handsome, he certainly did.

I always felt that something was missing in my life and I had an emptiness that relationships could not fill. There was a time when Jamie was just a baby and we were renting Grandma and Grandad Currie's house in Griffith. They had sold the farm and bought a house in Griffith until Grandad's death in 1970. Then Grandma went to live with Mum and Dad and my Auntie Ruth and Uncle John alternatively. The Mormons came knocking. They seem to have a good story to tell and I invited them in and they gave me their story using a flannel graph chart, a visual aid used to tell a story. When they started on about their prophet Joseph Smith, I knew that wasn't right and so the next time they came, I wouldn't answer the door to them. They eventually stopped coming. They believe that Jesus was a good man, but not God who came to earth as Jesus Christ. Then, a few years later, I was having singing lessons with a lady who was a Baha'i. They had a guru that they believed in but I knew this wasn't Christianity. I guess I must have learned something from going to the meetings with my grandparents.

The Other Woman

Then there came a night that was to change our lives irrevocably. It was the annual debutantes' ball which was held at the local Yoogali Club. It was that night that Marcus met a young debutante. He was to dance with her almost all night. That was to be the beginning of their affair which lasted for the rest of our marriage resulting in two children to her. We were living in a house in Canal St at that time.

We then moved in to a house along Griffin Ave and lived there for several years. Marcus was a panel beater/spray painter and he eventually opened his own business. I then fell pregnant again and gave birth to Matthew on March 3rd, 1972 after a short labour. Matthew weighed 8lb 14 ½ ozs. He was a beautiful baby with olive skin and dark hair. He was a bonny baby and very good, that is until he began toddling and then he was very mischievous. There was only 21 months between the boys and so I had my hands full most of the time.

Mum and dad were back living near Griffith as Dad was working on a farm not far out of town. When Matthew was only a few months old, I took the boys with me to Melbourne as I just couldn't take the abuse from Marcus anymore. I had a little Morris Minor and I drove it all the way to Frankston to where my cousin Barbara and her partner lived. My uncle and great aunt also lived not far away from her. My Aunt was my grandfather's youngest sister Ruth. Marcus came looking for me and he took Jamie back to Griffith and so I had to return to him. I left him again sometime later and this time I left the boys with my parents and stayed with my uncle and aunt for a couple of weeks.

I met a friend of my cousin and went out with him a few times. We were never intimate but I had a crush on him as he showed me the love and affection I craved. I went back home and it was then that Dad told me that I had made my bed so I had to lie in it. So I never went to them for a long time after that.

Marcus continued to live a "single" life, going out regularly to the club or hotel. He never helped me with the boys and would not be seen out with me with them as he said it would "cramp his style". I remember getting an anonymous letter about the girl he'd met at the debutant ball, and the fact that she was living in Canberra and Marcus had been to Canberra for a weekend. I was also informed through an unsigned letter that she had given birth to a daughter just 8 months after I had given birth to my son Matthew. They continued their affair for most of our marriage.

In my 20s, I discovered a lump in my neck, and after going to see about it, It turned out that I had a cyst on my thyroid gland, sometimes called a goitre, can be caused by an under active thyroid gland. I had it removed and haven't had any problems with my thyroid since then. Mum also had part of her thyroid gland out later in life.

I had been on the contraceptive pill and it had given me some side-effects, so I decided to have an IUD inserted. It was known as the Lippes Loop, a plastic uterine device that is supposed to sit in the uterine cavity to stop pregnancy. So after going to the GP and having it put in, after 5 days of sharp pains, I decided to go and have it taken out. When the doctor went to remove it, it wasn't there. So he sent me for an x-ray and discovered that it had perforated my uterus and was floating around somewhere among my intestines. So I was admitted for an emergency laparotomy where they removed the IUD.

All went well until about two weeks later, I was doing the grocery shopping, when I felt something warm flowing down my legs. It seems that I had begun hemorrhaging and so an ambulance was called and I was taken to Griffith Base Hospital. I was to then spend four weeks in hospital with on again, off again bleeding which had at one time resulted in my stopping breathing from the large amount of blood loss. One of the nurses on duty gave me heart massage (CPR) and revived me. They tried all sorts of treatments to try to stop the bleeding. They even packed me up inside with gauze soaked in Iodine. Very painful. I'd stop bleeding for some time, so they'd get me up walking and it would start up again. I was eventually sent over to Wagga Wagga Base Hospital and the doctor there ordered complete bed rest to let the hole in my uterus heal up. It eventually healed and I returned home. My two boys were looked after by their father and his mother Gladys.

Lippes Loop Contaceptive Device

In 1962, Dr. Jack Lippes developed and inserted the first of what be came known as the Lippes Loop. It was a simple plastic device, which was pushed through an inserter tube just like the Coil and eventually came in different sizes, depending on if and how many times a woman had been pregnant. A string was once again attached which facilitated detection and removal. The Loop was so easy to insert, remove, and inexpensive, it's use took off and it quickly became the most popular and most copied IUD in the world. Within a few years there were all different kinds of IUDs – some successful and others having severe complications. (Source-www.reproductiveaccess.org)

Rose and Marcus

Chapter 7

Another Baby

> *Whatever is good and perfect is a gift coming*
> *down to us from God our Father, who created all*
> *the lights in the heavens. James 1:17 (NLT)*

Then in 1977 I found out that I was pregnant again. I had been trying to fall pregnant for quite some time as I thought that a baby might help our marriage. One morning I woke up to bleeding so Marcus called the ambulance and I was taken to hospital. It seemed that I had Placenta Praevia. This is a condition where the placenta is below the baby instead of behind so that as the baby grows, it puts pressure on the placenta and you can bleed to death. I was only twenty six weeks and I had to lay flat in hospital with complete bed rest. The plan was to fly me to Sydney to The Prince of Wales Hospital in Sydney until I had the baby, but I started to bleed heavily at twenty eight weeks so the doctor had to perform an emergency caesarean to save my life.

I had 14 bags of blood pumped into me by the time Belinda Jane was born. She was a tiny 1lb 14 ozs and only lived a few hours. She was put on a plane to be flown to Sydney to the Prince of Wales Hospital, but she died on the way. I never saw my baby girl. The local Anglican priest baptized her before she was put on the plane. Marcus' family were Anglican, but I put down that I was Presbyterian. The local Presbyterian pastor came to visit me regularly and was very helpful to me. He shared with me about how he and his wife had also lost a baby.

Placenta Previa

> The placenta is an organ that develops in the uterus during pregnancy. In most pregnancies, the placenta attaches at the top or on the side of the uterus. In placenta previa, the placenta attaches low in the uterus. The placenta might partially or completely cover the opening of the uterus, called the cervix. Placenta previa can cause severe bleeding in the mother before, during or after delivery. (Source- www.mayoclinic.org)

I was in hospital for five weeks as I had a huge haematoma where my tummy was cut and had to recover from the extensive blood loss. Marcus organized a funeral for our baby but I was too sick to go. I don't even know who went except that my parents and my uncle and aunt went and Marcus and his mother. We never discussed our loss and I don't know how Marcus felt about it. He was still having an affair with the same woman and I found out years later that they had another daughter and had adopted her out. I was out of hospital only for about five days when I was driving up town with a friend of mine when who should I come across in his car up the main street but Marcus and his mistress in a very tight embrace. We parked around the back of the park and I walked across and yanked open the door and let them both have it. They were both rather surprised I must say. I stayed at my friend's place that night and stayed there for a few more days. Of course, he came crawling back and begged me to go back to him. I was still quite weak and quite frankly, didn't know what to do, so I reluctantly went back.

Our marriage continued in much the same vein, drinking, abuse, infidelities. I craved love and affection and often had a crush on someone. I always fantasied about living happily ever after with someone who'd come and rescue me. But, Marcus was so controlling, it was never going to happen. One day he bought a gun home and he showed me and told me that he could shoot me with it and he'd probably only get 7 years for it. I told him that I would report him to the police if he didn't get rid of it. So he got rid of it. I do believe now that if I'd have stayed that he could easily have eventually killed me. With so much domestic violence today, there was a lot of it back then too. I was really afraid of him and knew that I somehow had to get out of there away from him.

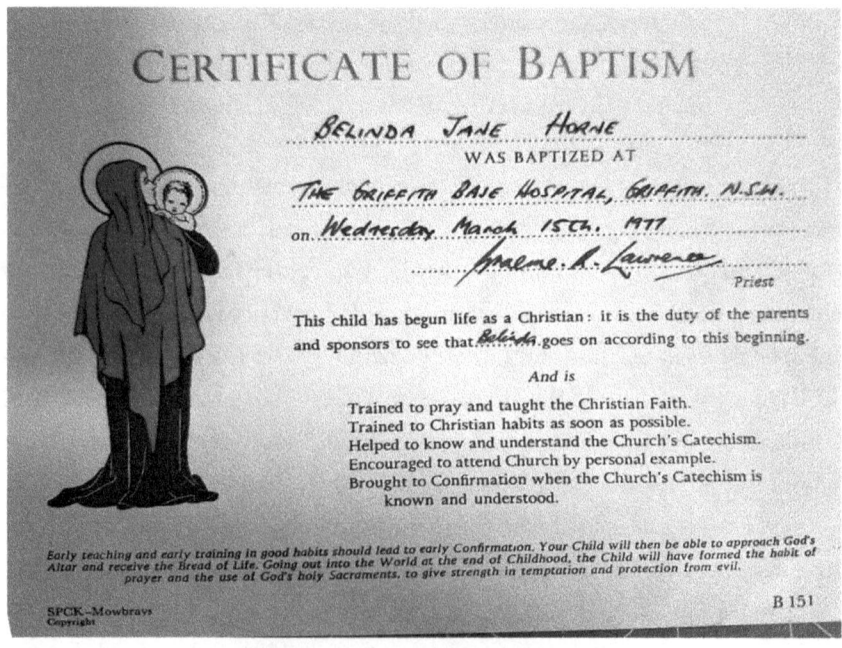

Belinda's baptism Certificate

Belinda's Grave

Little Angel

I had a little angel, a long, long time ago,
Although I never saw her, Oh how I loved her so.
I never held her in my arms in a soft caress,
Or kissed her sweet face gently, or held her to my breast.

(Chorus) But in my mind I see her, in my heart she'll stay,
And in my soul I feel her, she never went away.

She's up there with the Father, I know she's there to stay.
He has His arms around her and watches her each day.
Oh my darling little angel, you'll never leave my heart.
I know one day there'll come a day,
when we'll never be apart. (Repeat Chorus)

I had a little angel, a long, long time ago,
Although I never saw her, Oh how I loved her so.

Chapter 8

Leaving Home

The Lord is close to the brokenhearted; He rescues those whose spirits are crushed. Psalm 34:18 (NLT)

I went to see Marcus' mistress to ask her about her relationship with my husband. We sat down and had a cordial conversation about their relationship. Their daughter looked a lot like my son Matt, and Marcus had not paid any maintenance for her. The interesting thing about their affair, that when we did split up finally, they never ended up together and she married someone else! It was Matt who went to see her after Marcus had died and before he came up to Queensland to live. It was then that she told him about another baby that they had adopted out. He then told me. It was still a shock even after all the years had passed.

Things weren't much better over the next 12 months and I was still grieving the loss of my baby girl. One night after Marcus had been drinking, he came home and threw his dinner at me. I decided then that I had to leave, and this time leave for good. So over the next few days I packed clothes in bags and hid them around the house. By then my parents had given me a car and so one day, after Marcus went off to work, I packed the car and told the boys we were going on a holiday. I drove all the way to Adelaide where my brother and his first wife were now living with their son, Nathan. The car broke down half way over but I was lucky to be near a little town where a man had a mechanics workshop and he was able to get the part for the car for me. So we were on our way again and arrived safely at my brother's place.

My sister-in-law was a 7th Day Adventist and she knew someone who had a fully furnished house for rent. I was able to apply for the supporting parent's pension which had only recently come out during the Whitlam Government. So I had a place to live and money to support myself and my boys. I enrolled the boys into the local school at Port Noarlunga which was where the house was not far from the ocean. After picking the boys up from school each day, I befriended a man and his sister. The man had two little boys and we soon all became friends. I was attracted to this man and he was going back to Western Australia where he came from and wanted me to go with him. But it was too far away and I had planned on going up to Central Queensland to my older sister Esther's place to live.

In the meantime, Marcus was making his own plans on how to get me back. We had been to court for the custody hearing and I was granted temporary custody of the boys. Marcus was given access to see them and he and his mother came over and had the boys over to their motel room for an access visit. It was there that he found out where we were living.

A few weeks later he put his plan into action. One night we were asleep and I heard someone coming down the hallway and I thought that I was about to be attacked or raped. Someone put an Ether soaked cloth over my mouth and punched me in the eye. Ether is sometime used as an anaesthetic or as a solvent by mechanics. I screamed and then a voice said, "Shut up, it's only me." It was Marcus. In a way I was relieved as I thought it was going to be much worse. He then held the boys and I hostage in the house. He wouldn't let us out all day, and it was only when I said I'd think about going back with him if he would take the boys for a drive while I thought about it. As soon as he left, I went next door and called the police. They were there waiting for him when he returned. Poor little Matthew went crying up the road and tried to get away from the police. It was heart breaking and the boys were both crying. The police wanted to know if I wanted to press charges. I was really worried that if I did and he went to jail, that when he came out he would come and get me, so I said" no". He was free to go. He then went back to Griffith. So I went back to court to have his access visits stopped. The magistrate agreed and he was not allowed access until he went back to court to prove that he was fit to have them.

A few weeks later, Marcus and his mother came back to Adelaide and came around to my brother's place where I was visiting for the day. Matthew was outside playing with his cousin, Nathan, so Marcus grabbed Matt and they went back to Griffith. I was pretty distraught and so I went back to court and through Legal Aid, I was given a private investigator who drove me back to Griffith to get Matthew back. I had the paperwork which I took to the police station and they picked up Marcus and Matthew and from there we were able to take Matthew back with us. Marcus was crying, Matthew was crying, it was a pitiful scene. Matthew spent the whole drive back to Adelaide pinching me. I think he was traumatised from all that had occurred.

After that, I knew I had to get further away from him. So I packed up the car and drove up to Rockhampton to be near my sister Esther. When I think back now to all the chances that I took, I did things I would not even think of doing today. The car that I had was old and I don't even know how reliable it was, but it did get us there.

For several years, if I spoke about my life with Marcus to anyone, I would break out in a rash all over my face, my chest, and my arm and I would shake all over. So I made a conscious effort from then on not to talk about him and me. I realise now in hindsight that it was classic signs of anxiety. I also decided that I would no longer cry as I had cried so much during our marriage, I just didn't want to be that vulnerable again. It took me years before I let myself cry again. I do believe that it was about that time that I developed Irritable Bowel Syndrome (IBS) that has plagued me right up to the present day. I now know that it is a manifestation of anxiety.

Chapter 9

Queensland

> *I will be glad and rejoice in Your unfailing love,*
> *for You have seen my troubles, and You care about*
> *the anguish of my soul. Psalm 31:7 (NLT)*

My sister Esther lived on my cousin's farm in a caravan with her husband Winky and their four children, which was at a little village called Stanwell, not far out of Rockhampton. I felt really safe there and started to settle down a bit. The boys were enrolled in the local school at Stanwell. We lived in the house on the farm. My cousin also owned the local shop which had a house attached, so she lived there with her family.

It was there that I met a man whom I fell in love with in my quest for "Mr Right".. His name was Brian and he worked on the electrification of the railway which ran through Stanwell. This was in preparation for electrifying the rail lines for the coal trains to run from the mines through to Gladstone. He was tall, blonde, and good looking. He was very charming and there was an instant attraction between us. He had family in Griffith and so we had a lot in common. His mum and sister and his brother still lived there. He liked a drink but I didn't think much of it as he was a happy drunk. I later found out that his father was an alcoholic and was homeless, and lived under the huts at the railway station in Griffith. Within no time we were living together out at a little town called Gogango which was on the rail line to Gladstone.

We shared the house with two of Brian's mates, Bill and Rod. Rod played the guitar and it was then that Brian bought me my first guitar which I taught myself to play using a chord chart. The boys went to the local school which was within walking distance. I also had a job there as a cleaner. It was while we were living there that I had my first bout of knee problems. One day I woke up and my knee locked and would not straighten. I went to the local hospital at Rockhampton and I then had to go under anaesthetic and have it manipulated straight again.

I was then booked in for surgery to have it opened up and scraped out as there was piece of floating bone in the knee joint. In those days there was no arthroscopic surgery like there is today. The doctor surmised that I had had some sort of arthritis as a child and that the bits of cartilage had chipped off over the years. I had suffered many leg aches and cramps as a child but it was years later that I was diagnosed with having had a disease called Ostiochondritis Dissicans. I was to have two knee replacements in my 60s.

Ostiochondritis Dissicans

Osteo Condritis Dissecans Osteochondritis dissecans (os-tee-o-kon-DRY-tis DIS-uh-kanz) is a joint condition in which bone underneath the cartilage of a joint dies due to lack of blood flow. This bone and cartilage can then break loose, causing pain and possibly hindering joint motion. Osteochondritis dissecans occurs most often in children and adolescents. It can cause symptoms either after an injury to a joint or after several months of activity, especially high-impact activity such as jumping and running, that affects the joint. The condition occurs most commonly in the knee, but also occurs in elbows, ankles and other joints. Doctors stage osteochondritis dissecans according to the size of the injury, whether the fragment is partially or completely detached, and whether the fragment stays in place. If the loosened piece of cartilage and bone stays in place, you may have few or no symptoms. For young children whose bones are still developing, the injury might heal by itself. Surgery might be necessary if the fragment comes loose and gets caught between the moving parts of your joint or if you have persistent pain. (Source- www.mayoclinic.org)

Initially Brian and I were very happy living together and he really like my boys. They all got on well together and had lots of fun and adventures out at Gogango and then another little town called Dingo. Mum and Dad were not happy with me at all that I was living in sin. I had really hurt them this time. We then decided to move into town and found a house to rent at Emu Park. Brian worked out all week on the railway line and came home at the weekends. We then moved to Yeppoon and rented a house there. It was there that I fell pregnant, but I didn't know it at the time. We had planned this baby and I had gone off the pill to try to conceive. Then one night, Brian and his friends had been on a drinking binge all weekend and we had been down by the water where the men were drinking and partying on. I wanted to go home and so he got angry with me and went to put his fist through the car door as I tried to drive away. I had had enough of his obnoxious behaviour, so I drove home with the boys and packed up the car and drove to Brisbane. I felt so hurt and disappointed and I began to think that all men were the same.

I found a women's refuge and stayed there for a while until I moved in with a friend. Her husband had worked with Brian and she said we could stay with her. It was there that I found out that I was pregnant. I told Brian and he came down and we reconciled. We then drove up to Kingaroy and found a small place to rent just outside of Kingaroy. Brian was able to get a job at the new Tarong Power Station that was just starting up. We had no furniture but gradually got a few bits and pieces.

And Another Baby

We then found a house a bit closer to the job, and so we moved to "Blue Hills", Yarraman. The boys then moved to another school. It was whilst living there that I began to bleed at about 19 weeks into my pregnancy.

Marcus had been up to pick up the boys to take them back for a holiday as he had started to have visiting rights by then. Brian drove me in to Kingaroy Hospital and I was admitted. The doctor thought that if I would deliver the baby that it would die as I had placenta previa again. But the baby held on and I was transferred to Royal Brisbane Women's Hospital by ambulance, with a police escort through Brisbane. I was ordered to stay in bed to try to give the baby a better chance of growing and me not bleeding any further. I was given injections called Betamethazone to help mature the baby's lungs ready for delivery. I bled on and off until I was able hold on to thirty two weeks.

During the three months in hospital, Marcus brought the boys up to visit me, only to try to get me to sign papers to give him custody. I refused, he went home. Brian came to visit me twice in that time. It turned out that he had rolled the car whilst drinking and wrecked it so he had no way of coming to see me. The only visitors I had were some of Mum and Dad's friends who lived at Bribie Island. Also a 7th Day Adventist minister who visited after my sister-in-law told him about me. I enjoyed his visits. It was a lonely time.

At thirty two weeks I began to bleed heavily again so it was decided that I would have to have the baby delivered by caesarean section. This was a dangerous situation as I was in danger of bleeding to death. Dr Ivor Thomas was my surgeon and he delivered Robert Darryl on the 8th March, 1981. He was 4lb 6 ozs and had breathing difficulties. My uterus had split open on the operating table and I was still bleeding and was given over 8 bags of blood. I nearly had to go back for a hysterectomy but they decided not too when the bleeding finally ceased. I wanted the doctor to give me a tubal ligation but he said no, in case I wanted more children if my baby had died. I found out years later that Dr Thomas was a Christian.

Robert was placed in a humidicrib with fairly high oxygen to give him a chance at life. It was touch and go for the first forty eight hours, but he rallied and so it looked like he would survive. I was able to go home nine days later, on my birthday, 17th March, 1981. Brian came and picked me up and we had to leave little Robert there. Then after four weeks he had grown stronger and reached over 5 lbs so we were able to go and pick him up. I had to go into hospital for a couple of nights to learn how to feed him. He had to be able to drink a certain amount of milk each feed before I could bring him home. Premi babies have trouble sucking and so they have to be taught how. When we first went to have a look at him, there were 3 babies wrapped up in bassinets and we weren't sure which one was ours!

So, we were at last able to take him home to Yarraman. He was a good little baby and I used to lay him on my chest, skin to skin contact, now called kangaroo cuddles, a very popular thing to do with premi babies. Robert thrived and took his bottles well. He grew strong and put on weight. He was a bit behind in his milestones and didn't walk until he was 15 months.

Robert struggled at school and was diagnosed with dyslexia when he was about seven. He was very tall for his age and was always a head taller than the other kids in his class all the way through school. His father was tall but

Robert was eventually to grow even taller than his father. He was eventually diagnosed with schizophrenia at age nineteen.

Eventually Brian and I moved to Bundaberg and we found a house to rent on a sugar cane farm. Brian did have some work on a prawn trawler for a while. He was still drinking heavily and when Robert was only four months old, I left and drove down to Griffith. I stayed with Brian's sister for awhile, but I was very sick with a severe ear infection and Shingles. His sister looked after Robert but she didn't look after me very well. I eventually moved in with my brother and his first wife, who were now living in Griffith. Jamie and Matthew were living with their father, and his mother Gladys, in Griffith.

Brian eventually came down to Griffith and we were reconciled. I then went with him back up to Bundaberg. Things were good for some time. From time to time Brian would try to give up drinking but it didn't last. Then one day the police came to our place looking for Brian. Apparently, a women had reported him to the police for inappropriate behaviour. His car had supposedly broken down, and he was underneath it and she stopped to help him and he apparently said something inappropriate to her so she reported him. So he fled and the police searched the house and questioned me. I told them that he was on a prawn trawler.

Then I had to tell them that I'd lied and I didn't know where he was. He was hiding in the cane fields somewhere. They took my car for inspection, and after they'd left, he came and said he was going to catch a truck and go south. Then I never heard from him. So I sold all of our furniture to the local second-hand shop and packed up my personal belongings and had them sent to my parents place by truck. I then packed up my car, which had been returned to me, and set off for my parents place at Tullibigeal in N.S.W. With little Robert in the care, I only made it as far as Gympie as the car started leaking fuel. I stopped off at a caravan park and sold the car to a local wreckers, and then booked a flight to Sydney. We then caught a bus to West Wyalong and my parents came and picked us up.

Marcus eventually took out proceedings to get custody of Jamie and Matt. I was in no position to fight for them as I had nowhere to live and had a premi baby to look after, so I didn't contest the custody and they went back to live with Marcus and his mother. They were just nine and eleven. I will always regret not fighting for them.

Back Home

I only stayed at my parents who were now living back at Tullibigeal on a small farm, for a short while and then they drove me to Griffith so I could see Jamie and Matt. I eventually was able to rent a house on the farm in Griffith belonging to an Italian farmer. I stayed for some time and had a few casual relationships. I had a young man boarding with me to help with the rent.

I also had a severe gall bladder attack and eventually had to have my gall bladder out at Griffith Base Hospital. I had gallstones like gravel. I was in hospital for 2 weeks recovering. These days the gallbladder is removed by keyhole surgery. A good friend of mine looked after Robert for me.

I felt unhappy living in Griffith where Marcus was able to watch my every move so I decided to leave Griffith and move to Shoalhaven Heads where a good friend of mine was now living. The boys were still living with Marcus and his mother.

Before I left, one night Marcus' mother and Matt came up to my place and they both abused me and called me terrible names. I remember her saying, "You, I could write a book about you!." Well, I beat her to it! Marcus eventually met another woman, and Matt went to live with them at Darlington Point. Jamie stayed with his grandmother.

Chapter 10

Shoalhaven Heads

The Lord says, "And I will restore to you the years that the locust hath eaten" Joel 2:25 (KJV)

Money can be restored. Property can be restored - cars, paintings, old houses. Relationships can be restored. But one thing that can never be restored is time. Time flies and it does not return. Years pass and we never get them back. Yet here we find God promising the impossible. "I will restore the years that the locust has eaten." The immediate meaning of this promise is clear.

A division comes to a family and there is alienation from a loved one. Children grow up. And what might have been cannot be recovered. I know what it is to quietly endure a marriage in which love has been burning low for many years. I see a couple who are really in love and I say, "I wish I could be loved like that." Years have passed and there's no way I can get those years back. It feels like the locusts have eaten them.

The misdirected years. I had followed a path, but it didn't work out the way that I'd hoped it would. I made *many mistakes and wrong decisions and now I look back on my life and feel that I should have made a different choice.*

Often in my mind, and sometimes in conversations, I say, "How did I end up here?" And I find myself saying more and more, "If only... If only I hadn't done that... If only I hadn't married that person... If only I'd chosen a different path..." But the moment has passed. It's gone. I can't go back to it. I'm left with locust years. (Adapted from Open the Bible with Pastor Colin Smith)

After moving to Shoalhaven Heads near Nowra, I lived with my friend Jan and her family in a grannie flat. Robert started at the local school along with my friend's two little girls. I stayed there for probably 16 months or so. I had met a few different male friends and went out with them, but nothing serious. Matt wanted to come and live with me but he didn't want to go to school. I said he could stay but that he had to go to school. So he went back to his father's in Griffith.

Jamie came for a holiday and seemed to be doing okay. He excelled at school and was always top off his class. He'd started playing Australian Rules Football (AFL) and seemed to enjoy that. I was able to find a small cottage for rent and it was then that my friend Jan introduced me to some born again Christians, Syd and Debbie. My friend Jan said that she knew these people who'd be good for me. For a very long time I had a deep seated emptiness in my heart that I'd tried to fill with relationships. I thought that if I just met "Mr Right", I'd be happy and I wouldn't feel so empty anymore. I started to go to their home group meetings and it was there that I gave my life to Jesus Christ. I'd had a terrifying dream that the devil was trying to pull me in to the pit of hell. I shared this one night at home group and I became very emotional and knew that I needed to change my life, so I accepted Jesus Christ into my life as my Lord and Saviour, and it was then that my life began to change.

Coming to Faith

John 3:3 Jesus says, Most assuredly, I say to you, unless one is born again, he cannot see the Kingdom of God.

So I started to go to Syd and Debbie's church which was a charismatic church in nearby Nowra. I'd never been to a church like it. It was certainly different to the one I was brought up in. Everyone was so cheerful and enthusiastic! I found out that it was a Pentecostal Church. There was a small outreach at Shoalhaven Heads, so I decided to go to it as I didn't have to travel so far. This was a good fit for me as it was small and they were lovely people. I eventually was baptized in the local heated pool.

I felt that I was going well and that my life would now change. But I was still looking for "Mr Right" and was always attracted to someone or other. This was to bring me down and I fell into sin again.

Then my cousin Barbara passed away suddenly from a heart attack. Barbara's mother was my grandfather, Jack Haworth's sister, Ruth. She'd been living with her partner Allan (Butch) for about eighteen years. They'd never married and she'd never divorced her husband. Barbara and her first husband Stan had only been married a short time and they had a baby daughter that died of cot death. She and Butch met up and they became a couple and moved to Melbourne and then eventually to Clermont in Central Qld as Butch had a job in the mines. Barb was morbidly obese and she was only 38 when she died.

I'd sent Butch a sympathy card and invited him to come and stay anytime he was down my way. Four months later he called in to visit me and we became friends and he asked me to come up to live with him in Clermont. My sister and her family were also living there so I thought about it and decided to give it a shot. We were only platonic friends at first.

I had to talk to Jamie and Matt about it. So I went to Griffith to tell them of my decision. They didn't seem to mind, but I knew I'd miss them terribly and that it would be a long way away from them. I thought that maybe they were old enough to be without me. This wasn't to be the case.

Chapter 11

CLERMONT

> *Do not be unequally yoked together with unbelievers.*
> *For what fellowship has righteousness with lawlessness?*
> *And what communion has light with darkness?*
> *2 Corinthians 6:14 (NKJ)*

So I packed up all earthly belongings and put them on the train to Clermont and Robert and I caught the train to Rockhampton where Butch came in and met us as the train didn't go out to Clermont. We lived in a mining house with Butch and we both had separate rooms. Then I met a lovely lady one morning when I attended a morning tea at the local Salvation Army Church. Her name is Denise and we are still in contact today after all these years. I was still being drawn back to God and knew that I wasn't doing the right thing. Through my friend Denise, I met the pastor's wife of the local Assembly of God (AOG) church and she invited me to her church. I felt very at home there and told them all about my life and why I was living here with Butch. They were very supportive and I had some counselling with them and rededicated my life to the Lord.

I joined a music group and loved to join in playing the guitar with them. It was 1988 and there was a competition going for a song to do with the

Bi-Centenary. So I wrote a song called "Old Clermont Town" and I entered it into the competition and I won 2nd prize!

I was involved with the music team at church. The pastor talked to Butch and me about our situation and encouraged us to either separate or marry. Butch thought we should marry and so began our plans. I don't think I really loved him but he was a good man and I didn't think anyone would take me after they knew about my past. We had our wedding at the house and the pastor married us. He had a long talk with Butch and I think Butch must have made a decision for Christ, but he never ever told me that he did. It was hard on my other cousins, Barbara's sister Margaret and brother John, as it hadn't been that long since her death. My parents drove all the way up and so did Butch's parents and sister and husband. Jamie and Matt couldn't come up as it was a long way away. We had our honeymoon at Mackay and had a day at Brampton Island.

A Death In The Family

We were only married for two weeks when I received a phone call from Matt that his father, Marcus, had been killed in a car accident. Mat was living with Marcus and Brenda and her two children out at Darlington Point, Jamie was still living in Griffith with his Grandmother. Marcus was only forty years old and had been playing indoor cricket. He lived with his partner Brenda, her two kids, and Matt at Darlington Point, which was about 40 kms from Griffith. As Marcus drove home that night, it was assumed that he fell asleep at the wheel and hit a semi-trailer head-on. He was killed instantly. The unfortunate part about it, besides his death, was that he'd let his driving license lapse and so the trucking company sued his estate. A few weeks before his death, he'd taken out a life insurance policy, which helped the boys. Jamie was able to get into Uni in Canberra, and he bought his first car.

I was able to go down for the funeral and to support my boys. I left Robert with my sister at Clermont. I travelled down by bus. It was a big funeral as he was a very well-known person and had been involved in the local Rugby League team for many years. Matt wouldn't let me comfort him and so I sat with Jamie at the funeral. Matt was very distant from me and took his father's death harder than Jamie. I wanted them to come up to Clermont to live with me and Butch. But Butch didn't want them and they wanted to stay in Griffith. Jamie was in his last year of high school and wanted to go on to Canberra University. He was very bright and excelled at school. Matt just wanted to leave school and get a job. So I reluctantly went back to Clermont and left them there. Matt moved back in with his grandmother and Jamie. She was living at the time with her friend Geoff. She'd had a relationship with Geoff for many years and now he was sick so he moved in with her so she could look after him. Marcus' father Eric had passed away a few years earlier from pancreatic cancer. I knew when I arrived back in Clermont that I should never have married Butch. We had nothing in common and he reluctantly came to church with me.

Butch had friends in Albury, NSW that owned a scrap metal business. I wrote to the friend and asked him if he could offer Butch a job driving one of the scrap metal trucks. I had asked Butch if we could move down that way so I could be closer to the boys. He agreed as he wanted to get out of the mines. He had only one lung and suffered from Bronchiectasis which is a condition in which the lung's become damaged, making it hard to clear mucus. He'd had a car accident in his teens which resulted in a damaged lung. So he agreed and we made plans to leave Clermont.

Rose and Butch

Chapter 12

HOWLONG

> *The temptations in your life are no different from what others experience. And God is faithful. He will not allow the temptation to be more than you can stand. When you are tempted, He will show you a way out so that you can endure. 1 Corinthians 10:13 (NLT)*

We found a little old house to rent at a town called Howlong, just outside Albury. Butch had two cars but he forbade me to drive one of them to Griffith to see the boys. I had started a job at the local motel as a cleaner and so I saved up my pay and bought myself a little car. Butch was driving a truck to Melbourne and back picking up scrap metal. Our relationship was not close and there was no intimacy. I think he still missed Barbara and we married far too soon after her death. He didn't seem to know how to relate to me, and maybe I didn't know how to relate to him.

Robert was enrolled in the local state school and it was there that he was diagnosed with dyslexia. At that time, we'd heard about the coloured glasses that helped people with dyslexia. So we went to the optometrist that prescribed them and we found it did help Robert a lot. He can read but he has trouble with spelling. Not long after we arrived in Howlong I met a lady who was going to a local church. So we eventually became involved in the church, and we had home group at our house. But Butch would always sit in the kitchen when we had our Bible study in the lounge room. He didn't seem to enjoy the church experience at all. I then ran into an old school friend of mine, Rhonda, who was now living in Albury. We had been school friends and had lost contact after we'd both married. She had four daughters and had divorced her first husband and had remarried.

I then decided to leave Butch. I couldn't see a future for us. So I packed our things over a period of time and took them in to Rhonda's place in Albury and stored everything there. I then left him a note and moved in with her and her husband. Her daughter's had all left home by this. I haven't seen Butch to this day. He was to pass away in October, 2018. He had remarried and had been with Jenny for many years. He had heart and lung issues which were to take his life. I've always maintained contact with his sister Lyn who lives in Yenda, near Griffith.

I then received a letter from my brother Stan who was now living up on Bribie Island. My parents had retired up there to live and so my brother eventually moved there too. He said I was welcome to come up anytime and that he and Mum and Dad would support me and help me get back on my feet. I knew that I needed a new start in life and that I needed to put the past behind me.

I wrote this song called "Across the Border" about my life returning to Queensland.

ACROSS THE BORDER

1. I was sitting in a café down in Melbourne
Just thinking of the life that used to be
Got a ticket on the Greyhound and all my bags are packed
I'll soon be heading north to the sunshine, sand and sea.

2. As we travelled up the New England Highway
As we crossed over the great dividing range
The cattle are grazing and all the birds are singing
The land has come alive again drenched from the summer rains.

Chorus 1

As I get a little closer I can see the bougainvillea
And the sugar cane in northern New South Wales
The breeze is gently blowing through the pretty frangipani
The border's getting closer, I can see a new life waiting there for me.

3. then we finally made it across the border
I can see the Gold Coast, sunshine, sand and sea
I think I'll go a little further on up to Far North Queensland
As I put the past behind me and at last I know I'm free.

Chorus 2

As I get a little closer I can see the bougainvillea
And the sugar cane is blowing in the breeze
I can smell the sweet perfume of the pretty Frangipani
Now that I'm across the border I can see, there's a new life waiting there for me.
End:- Now that I'm across the border I can see
There's a new life waiting there for me.

Back to Queensland

I sold my car and put all of my belongs on the train and Robert and I flew up to Brisbane. My parents lived just off Bribie Island at a little village called Ningi. They had been able to rent a house across the road from them for us to move into. They had furnished it for me and everything was there for us to move straight in. This was a real blessing. I enrolled Robert into the Bribie Island State School. I was able to find a job at the local RSL club as a waitress. Mum minded Robert for me while I was at work. Dad bought a little second-hand car for me so I could get around. I started up a payment plan to pay my parents back for all they'd done for me. I eventually paid back everything.

I found it very claustrophobic living across from Mum and Dad, and it was there that I had a nasty falling out with my father. He and Mum were interfering in my life and I felt that at forty years of age, this was not on. So Dad came over to say something to me one day and I lashed out at him. I'd never been game to stand up to my father and so this was the first time in my life that I spoke back to him. I was angry and I told him that I had a right to my own life and didn't need him and Mum running it for me. I eventually found a small cottage at Godwin Beach which was not far from Ningi. Mum was not at all pleased with me moving and she didn't speak to me for 3 weeks! She sent over a list of all Dad's good points to show me that he was not all bad. Moving was a good thing and Mum still minded Robert for me while I worked at the RSL. In the mean time, I had applied for a Deparment of Housing unit on Bribie Island and this eventually came up and Robert and I moved there. I had also started a job at the local caravan park.

Sometime after, Dad had a heart attack and ended up in hospital. When I went in to see him with Mum, I told him that I loved him, and he started to cry. He said to me, "I didn't think you children ever loved me." Mum said to me, "Don't tell him that, you've made him cry!" I did feel an overwhelming love for my father that I had never felt before. I had been praying to God to help me to love my father and I believe that my heavenly Father had helped heal the wounds and hurts from the past and showed me another side to my father. Dad later passed away in 2006 from a brain haemorrhage. My brother, my sisters and Mum were all with him when he passed away in hospital. He had a graveside service at Tallowood Cemetery in Deception Bay. There were many relatives and his church friends in attendance. My brother Stan's children all came and was reconciled with them after not seeing them for several years. This was a special time for my brother Stan.

The unit we lived in on Bribie Island was not the greatest environment as we had some very unsavoury neighbours. One particular woman lived next door and she had many fights and altercations with her girlfriend who sometimes stayed over. They were eventually kicked out and a much nicer young woman moved in. We heard later on that one of them murdered the other one and was given a life sentence for it.

In 1994, I had a hysterectomy due to fibroids and adenomyosis which occurs when the tissue that normally lines the uterus (endometrial tissue) grows into the muscular wall of the uterus (Source: www.mayoclinic.org). It was such a relief to have it dealt with as I suffered from very heavy periods for so long.

Eventually, Jamie and Matt came up to Brisbane to live. Jamie had graduated from Canberra University as a computer analyst and found a job in Brisbane. He found a unit at Strathpine which wasn't far from me. He and Megan partnered over 20 years ago and they now live just outside Morayfield with their menagerie of ducks and guinea pigs..

Matt moved to the Gold Coast and did some modelling for a time. He then met Phionna and they had Bailey and Lacey-Jane and split up when the children were small. He then met Charli and they had Evi and Isla and split up several years later. Phionna married and had two more children, Julius and Ruby, who call me Grandma Rose. I have a great relationship with both Phionna and Charli and I see my grandchildren regularly. Matt and I are estranged at the moment, but my prayer is that we will be reconciled and that God will heal him from the hurts of the past. Bailey recently did a two year working holiday in Whistler in Canada. A great experience for a young man. He lives with his Mum and has a job as a night manager at a tavern. Lacey is studying and lives in Brisbane and I see her from time to time. We have a special bond. The children's mothers always ensure that I see the grandchildren and keep in contact. I love all of my beautiful grandchildren and I thank God for them.

Back to Church

I enjoyed my time living on Bribie Island. I was feeling the need to get back to church. I felt that I had not done right by God and needed to get back to living right. I had had a few casual relationships while I was at Bribie, men I'd met at the country music club, though nothing serious. I remember looking in the local paper every week to see what churches were around.

I found an ad for the local Assembly of God Church (AOG) on Bribie Island and decided after the first of January, 1991, that I would start attending church again. I rededicated my life to the Lord and started to have counselling with the pastor and his wife. This was very helpful and I began to understand where the root of some of my behaviour came from. I decided that I would have nothing to do with men and relationships again and I determined that I would not put myself in any situation that would tempt me again. I stayed true to this for 7 years as I healed from the past and became involved in the church. I joined the music team, Bible Study group, home group and I made new friends in the church.

Chapter 13

My Brother Stan

*A friend is always loyal, and a brother is born to
help in time of need. Proverbs 17:17 (NLT)*

My brother Stan had become an alcoholic over the years and was an interstate truck driver. He was married to Charmaine and they had 4 children, two girls and two boys. Charmaine and I were best friends and she was a great support to me over the years. Over the period of their marriage, his drinking became more and this put a strain on their marriage. They were now living on a farm at Lake Cargelligo in NSW. It all came to a head and somewhere through it all, he found himself at Alcoholics Anonymous (AA). He stopped drinking, but the marriage was in trouble, and Charmaine eventually took the children and left him. It was after this that Stan moved to Tullibigeal and stayed with my uncle and aunt for some time, then he eventually moved up to Bribie Island where Mum and Dad were now living.

He found an Alcoholics Anonymous (AA) group there and attended meetings religiously. His children were still down in NSW and there was a lot of animosity between him and his wife and trouble getting the children up to Bribie Island to spend time with their father. In the end, the stress became too much for him and so a friend at AA, his sponsor, advised him to cut ties with his children until they'd grown up. So he wrote each of them a letter to tell them that he didn't want to see them anymore. They were pretty devastated, especially the girls. The older boy Nathan had already left home and was at an Agricultural College at Yanco. He eventually came up to Queensland to live near his father. Stan had also suffered from severe depression and anxiety for many years and so he couldn't take a lot of stress. I think that his depression and anxiety were a result of the accident when he was just 15 when he ran over a little girl and she passed away.

He'd also met up with an old friend from Tullibigeal, Joanne. He brought her and her three children up to Bribie Island where they set up house together. They seemed happy and Stan had a job driving buses for a local Brisbane Bus Line. Eventually, Stan and Joanne were married. Joanne's oldest son was a very troubled young boy after having had a number of step-father's in his life and now another one. This caused a lot of stress in their marriage. Then Joanne decided that she had been an alcoholic and started going to AA meetings too. Before that, she'd being attending AL ANON, a support group for friends and families of the alcoholic. So, the marriage didn't last, she met someone else at AA and she and Stan split. This devastated Stan and he quickly slid into a depressive episode. Stan was deep down, a very sensitive man. He and I had a very close bond. He told me later that he had a tree picked out where he was going to hang himself as he couldn't take any more hurt in his life. Thankfully, he never did do it.

Stan moved in with me after he had split from Joanne, but he was terribly unhappy, and very depressed. Then he decided to move up to Yeppoon to live with our older sister Esther and her husband. There he found a job driving the bus from Yeppoon to Rockhampton. It was there that he met Jan, who used to catch the bus to Rockhampton to work every day. They struck up a friendship and so began another chapter in Stan's life.

Stan and Jan eventually married and they moved to the Northern Territory to manage the Tilmouth Roadhouse. They then moved to an Aboriginal Community called Yuendumu, about 3 hours' drive from Alice Springs, literally in the middle of nowhere! There they managed the store with another couple. More about that later.

My brother Stan passed away in October 2017, just after I had returned from my Christian Women Communicating International (CWCI) Safari to NSW. We were able to fly up to Ravenshoe in Qld to see him, and we arrived the night before he passed away from lung cancer and other lung complications. It was so awful to see him unable to breathe, even with oxygen. I am sorry we didn't get up there sooner. His body was taken down to Rockhampton for burial at Emu Park which was where he and his wife Jan had intended moving to. It was a beautiful graveside service. Stan had accepted the Lord Jesus as his Saviour many years ago. He and Jan attended the local Ravenshoe Uniting/Anglican Church. Jan eventually sold the house and moved to Emu Park where she now lives with her brother Archie. Stan leaves behind four children from his first marriage to Charmaine. Nathan, Aimee, Tammie, and Aiden and 6 grandchildren (and 1 deceased). I keep in contact with Stan's children from time to time and Nathan lives close by so I see him and his family more often.

Stan's eldest son Nathan, and his wife Christine have two children, Flynn and Ella, and they had baby Jon who was born sleeping. This happened just before my brother Stan passed away. It was a very sad little funeral. Nathan and Christine's other two children had painted pictures over Jon's little coffin. It broke my heart when I saw Nathan carry that little coffin into the chapel. I didn't get to go to my daughter's funeral, so in a way, it was probably what it would have been like.

Aimee and her husband Greg have two children, Beau and Elody, Tammie is married to Zane who has adult children, Aiden is married to Hosanna, and he has Lilly and Lake and Hosanna has 3 children. Their mother Charmaine is married to Ray and he has two adult children.

Stan and I had a close bond as we had a similar life and similar heartaches. We both became Christians many years ago which really helped both of us with our past traumatic experiences. Stan had a very tender heart, and was a very funny man. He had a way of telling stories that would keep you captivated and in stitches of laughter. He is so greatly missed. He could tell so many funny stories of growing up with our cousins, especially he and our cousin Ronnie. They did get up to a lot of mischief.

Song for my brother Stan

I wrote a song which was originally about my own situation with my two eldest sons, and then I realised that it was actually a song about my brother, and the separation of his wife and eventual separation from his children. It's called "No-one Will Ever Take Your Love From Me".

No-one Will Ever Take Your Love From Me

1. They came into our lives as little treasures
They were the tie that binds for all to see
We'd look into their eyes and see our future
And all our hopes and dreams there'd ever be.

2. And then our world came crashing down around us
Our hopes and dreams have flowed into the sea
Our little treasures now are used as weapons
The tie that binds is severed permanently.

The Woman at the Well

(Chorus)
But my darlings, I will always love you
Don't forget, you mean the world to me
I'll carry you inside my heart forever
No-one will ever take your love from me.

3. I believe the Lord will heal your sorrow
He can even mend a wounded heart
Just remember that I will always love you
No-one can ever take you from my heart.

4. I know one day the Lord will re-unite us
And we'll forget the years we've been apart
Just remember the Lord and I both love you
Together we can make a brand new start. (Chorus)

Stan and Jan

Stan and Charmaine

Chapter 14
Yuendumu N.T.

I had a friend, Judy, who lived at Godwin Beach, near where we had lived before. She wanted to rent her house out and so Robert and I moved back there after we left the Department of Housing unit. Robert caught the bus to school. He then started High School and struggled a lot and hated going to school. He was bullied because of his dyslexia and I think the fact that he was a head taller than the other kids in his class, more was expected of him. So I decided to home school him with the ACE program, Accelerated Christian Education. This worked fairly well for a time until we moved to the Northern Territory.

We'd only been there a few weeks when I received a phone call from my brother Stan. He and Jan had moved to Yuendumu, the Aboriginal Community in the N.T., as I mentioned earlier. He said that there was a job going in the community take-away store and would Robert and I like to come and he would give Robert a job in the store. Robert by then was 14, so he was old enough to leave school. I thought about it and talked it over with Mum and Dad. Dad was not in favour of us going as he'd expected me to be there for him and Mum in their old age. Mum thought it was a great opportunity. I had to quickly make up my mind or the job would be offered to someone else.

So, within a week, I'd packed up all our belongings and put them into storage, surrendered my two lovely cats to the RSPCA, and Robert, myself and our little dog, Taffy, were winging our way to Alice Springs. Dad wouldn't even kiss me goodbye at the airport! Taffy was a little tan Chihuahua, and we were very attached to him. We only intended staying for a year. As it turned out, we lasted 5 months!

When we arrived at Yuendumu, I think we suffered from culture shock! We couldn't believe what we saw. Robert took one look and said, "And you left all your friends for this!" There was litter blown up against all the fences in the township and rubbish was everywhere. It was just red dirt, hardly a tree or blade of grass. There were humpies and fibro houses which the government had built for the Aboriginals, some were broken down, smashed windows, doors off and many of the people there slept in their beds outside in their front yards. It was such an eye opener. You don't really understand from TV documentaries until you actually go there.

History of Yuendumu

Yuendumu is located within the Yuendumu Aboriginal Lands Trust area on traditional Anmatyerr and Walpiri land and includes numerous outstations. It was established in 1946 by the Native Affairs Branch of the Australian Government to deliver rations and welfare services. In 1947 a Baptist mission was established there. Population 687 (2011 census), located 293km (182 miles) from Alice Springs. In 1955 many of the Walpiri people had settled in the town. Today, some of the services and facilities available in Yuendumu include three community stores, Yuendumu mediation Centre, school, airstrip, swimming pool, the Warlukurlangu art centre, An Aboriginal media organisation (PAW Media), a church, an elderly people's program, women's centre and safe house. Yuendumu hosts its annual sports weekend the first week of August. The event includes football, basketball and softball competitions, attracting teams from other communities around the region. There is also a "Battle of the Bands" night which showcases local bands. (Source: www.wikipedia.org).

I started in the take-away store and Robert was put to work as a storeman in the store. Then my brother asked me if I knew anyone who would like to work in the takeaway with me and I thought of my friend Judy whose house I'd rented in Godwin Beach. She said yes and so she was also flown out to Alice Springs. I lived in a little one bedroom house and Robert had a relocatable room off the house. There was no room for Judy so the manager bought a caravan from Alice Springs and had it brought out and it was parked in the driveway of my little house.

Judy and I ran the takeaway together and it was great to have a friend out there as it was such an isolated and desolate place. It was great experience though, and Robert was taught some skills which would help him to get work when we came back home from Yuendumu.

There was the little Baptist Church that Robert, Stan and Jan, and I attended. Stan had become a Christian some time before and Jan was raised as an Anglican. There was pastor and his wife who took the services and they also had a very wide area to service. So they travelled a fare bit to provide services in other communities.

There was a lot of spiritual darkness at Yuendumu. Much witchcraft and strange happenings. Stan and Jan felt uneasy in the house that they were living in and Stan asked me if I'd come and pray through the house as he felt that there were evil spirits there. So we prayed through the house, through each room and Stan said it felt so much better after that.

> *The Lord will keep you from all harm and watches over your life. The Lord keeps watch over you as you come and go, both now and forever. Psalm 121: 7-8. (NLT)*

My brother Stan and his wife Jan, suspected that the manager and his wife were stealing from the store. So Jan reported them to the powers that be and the auditors were sent in to investigate. We were all sent in to Alice Springs while this investigation took place. This couple were found guilty and were given the sack. They moved on to another community and found work again. I decided we needed to get out of there. I found the isolation too much and I missed home. Robert was also very popular with the young Aboriginal girls. One of the elders came to me and warned me that if Robert touched any of their girls, he could be speared, as they had partners picked out for them. I decided then that it was time to get out. I contacted Robert's father in Victoria and asked him to take Robert for a while. He agreed and so I put Robert on a plane to Melbourne to go be with his father Brian for awhile and he stayed down there for a few months.

Stan and Jan eventually left Yuendumu and found work at another community at Finke.

Homesick

I then decided to fly to Cairns and stay with my Auntie Jean, my father's sister, and Uncle Bob who lived at Ravenshoe on the Atherton Tablelands as I hadn't seen them for many years. Auntie Jean and my cousin Jenny came and picked me up from the airport. I am very like my auntie and we look more like mother and daughter than with my own mother! They were happy to have me and "Taffy", my little dog. I stayed with them for a couple of weeks and then I rented a caravan at the local caravan park. I met a woman and her brother. They had a back packers hostel which was on the local steam train rail line. This was a great tourist attraction for the area. The train would pull in to the back packers and the lady who ran it would sell Devonshire teas for any passengers on the train. I went out a few times with the lady's brother and enjoyed my time there with my aunt and uncle. I stayed for about seven weeks, bought a little car and then drove back to Ningi to Mum and Dad's. They were happy that I'd come back. I then found a unit to rent in nearby Morayfield. Robert then wanted to come back and so I arranged for him to come home as he wasn't happy at his father's as he didn't like his father drinking.

I found another job at a take away food shop in the nearby shopping centre, and they also had a bakery and Robert was given a job there. This worked out well for both of us. I started attending a small Assembly of God church at Beachmere which was run by the pastor of the AOG at Bribie Island, so I felt that I fitted in there and knew a number of people.

The Lord Jesus Christ has changed my life. He's forgiven me for all the wrong things that I've done. He has filled that emptiness that I have had in my heart for so many years. He loves me and He died for me. I started to remember the Bible verses that I had learned as a child, and the old hymns from going to the meetings came back to me. I began to write gospel songs about what the Lord has done for me and how He has changed me. I can't imagine my life without Him now.

I did a lot of song writing during my time on Bribie Island. These songs I was able to record many years later.

> *John 10:27-28, Jesus says, "My sheep hear My voice, and I know them, and they follow me: And I give unto them eternal life; and they shall never perish, neither shall any man pluck them out of My hand."*

Chapter 15

VICTOR JAMES SOPHIOS

> *I was in prison and you came to visit me… I tell you the truth, whatever you did for one of the least of these brothers of mine, you did for Me. Matthew 25:36,40 (NLT)*

I then decided to attend the Country Gospel Music Club where I used to go before I left for Yuendumu. I had met a musician there before I went away. His name was Vic Sophios and he was a lead guitarist and singer. He had joined the clubs' "Good News Country Band" as their lead guitarist. We met up again and there was an attraction between us. We started to sing together and we found that our voices blended well together in harmony. He was divorced and had two young children, Emma and Matthew. He was an Australian born Greek, both his parents were born in Greece, his mum came to Australia as a toddler, his dad later on as an adult.

It wasn't long before we became an "item" and started to spend a lot of time together getting to know one another. I was attending the small AOG church at Beachmere and Vic was a member of the Lawnton Salvation Army and he lived at Albion with his elderly mother as his father had passed away years earlier. The children lived with their mother Janet, and Vic had them every second weekend. He was a taxi driver and was also attending Bible College.

After about six months, Vic proposed and asked me to marry him. We then purchased a house at Petrie, just north of Brisbane. Robert and I lived there until my marriage to Vic on the 3rd May, 1997. We were married at the Salvation Army by the Envoy, John Tatters. I had begun attending the same church as our relationship progressed. Vic's daughter Emma was our flower girl, and my son Jamie gave me away. We had a short honeymoon up at Caloundra on the Sunshine Coast.

We settled into our life at Petrie and I eventually got a job at the local bakery, just a short walk from our house. Robert began a course at an agricultural college which was hard for him as he didn't do too well. He had to catch two trains to get there. But he did finish the twelve month course He got on well with Vic's children initially, but then they seemed to fall out. Vic's son Matthew came to live with us full time and I think there were some jealousies between him and Robert.

Vic finished Bible College and he then joined a Prison Chaplaincy group called "Inside Out Chaplaincy". He began to visit prisoners at the local Woodford prison, every second Saturday. He built up friendships with several of the prisoners there.

Vic and I sang around other churches and he also loved to preach as he had a real heart for evangelism. So we had many opportunities to sing and share at different churches and of course, singing at the Country Gospel Club. We had also changed churches and began attending an Independent Baptist Church at Deception Bay. Vic was given the opportunity to preach there from time to time.

Then one day, Vic and Robert had a physical altercation over something trivial. I didn't know what to do about it, so I thought maybe some time down with his father again might be good for him. I sent him down to Melbourne again and his father picked him up. He stayed there for a few months until some strange behaviour emerged. He had found a job in at Shepparton at an Italian restaurant and so his father rented him a caravan at the local caravan park so he didn't have to go and drop him and pick him up each shift as he lived out of town with his girlfriend. Robert seemed okay for a time and then each time I spoke to him on the phone, he was behaving rather strangely. Vic and I decided that he should come home. So we arranged with Brian to fly him home. He then had a job at Hungry Jack's fast food restaurant when we noticed changes in is behaviour.

A serious diagnosis

At the beginning of 2000, Vic started to complain about feeling a bit unwell when he ate or drank. He seemed to have gastric reflux and found it hard to get food down. So, he went to the doctor and he was given reflux medication but that didn't seem to help at all. So he went back to the doctor and he ordered an endoscopy. The day he had the endoscopy, the doctor advised him to get back to his GP as soon as possible as he could hardly get the endoscope down Vic's oesophagus. Vic was diagnosed with cancer of the oesophagus. He then had to have an MRI scan and it was found that the cancer had metastasized into his liver.

We then had to see surgeons at The Royal Brisbane and Women's Hospital to see what could be done. But, it was really too late to do anything. The doctors thought he'd had it at least three years for it to be at the stage it was at. He could have had his stomach out and they would have then joined his oesophagus up to his bowel, but Vic didn't want that. He thought that he could fight it by eating healthy foods and juices. But that was like shutting the gate after the horse had bolted.

We went to see Vic's Uncle Jim, whom he was very close to. He and his wife Linda, decided that we should fight this and they came over to our place and built us a vegetable garden. We tried all sorts of so called cancer cures. People came out of the woodwork with their cancer cures. We did try a few like Noni Juice and also a South American Indian concoction that I had to boil up. We borrowed a juicing machine and juiced all sorts of fruit and veg. But the whole trouble was, Vic couldn't keep anything down. The cancer had almost blocked his oesophagus and so he had difficulty swallowing food, let alone juice.

Vic woke me up one night and said to me, "I'm going to die." A verse from the Bible came to us from the Book of Job in the Old Testament. *Though He slay me, yet will I trust Him. Job 13:15 (KJV)*. We believe that God is Sovereign and He is in control of our lives. Then we wondered how we would ever get through this and at first we were in denial and believed that we could beat it. But as Vic became sicker and he began to lose more weight, it became apparent that the Lord had chosen not to heal him, and we had to accept that he was going to die.

Around the same time as this was happening, Robert started showing signs of a mental illness. So I sent him to the doctor and he referred him to a psychiatrist who diagnosed him with Paranoid Schizophrenia. So began the long journey of mental illness and trying to get the right medication for him. He was just nineteen.

We were also trying to battle with Vic's illness and praying for a miracle and that he would be healed. Vic continued preaching and we still did some singing together. He began to lose a lot of weight as he couldn't keep anything down. He had to give up his taxi driving and I gave up my job at the bakery to care for him. We were able to access a small superannuation fund that Vic had. It kept us going. Vic's son Matthew was still living with us. It was hard on him, and his daughter Emma, to see their father getting worse.

Eventually the doctors decided he could have a stent put down his oesophagus to try and open it up so he could eat. The trouble was, the stent moved out of place and he had to go back in and have another one put in, as once they're in, they can't come out. It didn't seem to help much so they thought they'd put another stent further past his duodenum. He went in for that and he never came home. He was in extreme pain and was moved to palliative care at the Prince Charles Hospital. He passed away two weeks later on the 31st August, 2000.

Vic's sister and her husband had been in Greece for an extended holiday visiting family members. I did tell Vic that he needed to ring his sister and tell her of his condition. He did let her know and so they made plans to come home. While Vic was in hospital, I asked him if he could just hang on until his sister Vacelia and her husband arrived back. They made it the day before he passed away. Vic's brother John and his wife Michelle, his mother, his Uncle Jim and Linda, and my son Matthew and myself were all there as he passed away. Vic's ex wife Janet and their children came in to say goodbye to him the night before. No more pain and suffering, he was now in the presence of the Lord Jesus Christ, his Saviour whom he loved. He knew where he was going and wasn't afraid, but he didn't look forward to the actual dying process. The doctors asked him if he wanted to be put into a coma for the dying process, and he agreed.

It was a sad time as Vic and I had so many plans for the future. Vic trusted the Lord right until the end. We had the funeral service at the Pine Rivers Salvation Army and John Tatters, the Envoy for the church and our pastor from the Deception Bay Independent Baptist Church, Elmo Parish, shared the funeral service. The church was full to overflowing and several men from the Prison Chaplaincy, Inside Out Chaplaincy, that Vic was involved in, spoke. When he passed away, the prisoners gave me a lovely card that some of them had signed. There were some lovely comments on it as to how Vic had helped them and what he'd meant to them. I shared about our life together. Emma and Matthew came with their mother Janet. Jamie and my son Matthew and his then partner Phionna and their little kids Bailey and Lacey, who was just a baby, came. Robert of course was there. He was pretty upset that Vic had died. Vic had been a great encouragement to Robert's spiritual life. Vic was buried at the Pine Rivers Cemetery at Albany Creek, a lovely cemetery with lots of gum trees. Vic's elderly mother, who had a mental illness, was very upset at her son passing away. She actually passed away herself just six weeks after Vic after suffering a heart attack. This was hard on Vic's brother and sister, John and Vacelia. Vic's ex-wife Janet was to pass away 2024 from Louie Body dementia, a terrible disease.

Rose and Vic

Chapter 16

Bible College

> *I will be your God throughout your lifetime - until your hair is white with age. I made you, and I will care for you. I will carry you along and save you. Isaiah 46:4 (NLT)*

By this time I was fifty one years old so I decided to sell the house in Petrie and I had some things done to it first. I painted it inside and I had a fence and gates put up around the property. It was around the time of the property market boom and so I waited a little while and I managed to sell the house for a nice profit. I bought a small three bedroom cottage at Deception Bay for a good price. I had started going to Redcliffe Christian Assembly (now Mueller Community Church) in Rothwell and they had also just started up a brand new Bible College, Mueller College of Ministries (MCM). I decided to enrol at the Bible College, so moving over to Deception Bay meant I was a lot closer to the college and the church. Rothwell and Deception Bay are on the beautiful Redcliffe Peninsula. The church also had a school and a retirement village, Peninsula Palms, on the campus and in 2002, they had built and opened up an aged care facility. I applied for a position there as a Diversional Therapist and was successful in becoming a part-time Carer and Diversional Therapist. I job-shared with another lady,

Judy, and we worked well together. I had to train as a Carer and Diversional Therapist, so for the next several years I did courses by correspondence. I achieved a Certificate 4 in Community Service and Certificate 4 in Aged Care and also a Diploma of Diversional Therapy. I wasn't able to finish my studies at Bible College as I had to study for my new job. I loved this job and I was able to use my musical abilities during my time there, playing piano and also singing and playing my guitar.

So I was involved in the lifestyle activities at the facility which was called Peninsula Palms Residential Care Facility. I worked there until I retired at the end of 2010. My right knee had been troubling me since the first operation on it in 1980. It was now bone on bone, so I had a knee replacement in early 2010, just before my 60th birthday. It was pretty traumatic, and I had issues with it afterwards, as it wouldn't bend far enough. So I had to go back in and have a manipulation under anesthetic. It was much better after that, but it has never been the greatest.

I continued working for the rest of that year even though I found it difficult on my knee. My other knee was starting to give me issues too, so I thought it was time to retire. In 2015 I had my left knee replaced and this was a very successful operation.

I then began singing around nursing homes and aged care facilities for the next 9 years. I enjoyed this very much, playing guitar and singing the old songs that the residents enjoyed. I also began volunteering as well, and played the piano for singalongs at my old work place.

I wrote a song and put it to music taken from Psalm 98.

> *O Sing to the Lord a new song; sing to the Lord, For He has done marvellous things.*
> *Shout joyfully to the Lord all the earth, break forth into song, rejoice and sing.*

Sing to the Lord with the violin, with the harp and the sound of a hymn.
With trumpets and the sound of a horn, Sing joyfully before the Lord our King. (Psalm 98).

Chapter 17
ANOTHER WEDDING

*Love never gives up, never loses faith, is always
hopeful, and endures through every circumstance.
1 Corinthians 13:7 (NLT)*

*I*n 2005 I met up with an old friend, Doug Alexander. Yes, I know what you're thinking! His wife Robyn had passed away after a long illness from a lung condition and he was working at Peninsula Palms. We became good friends and the residents did a bit of match making. Doug had 3 children, Trevor, Trudy and Sarah. Eventually, we decided to marry. It had been five years since Vic's death and over two years since Doug's wife, Robyn's death. It was a bit hard on Doug's daughters, Sarah and Trudy, but I eventually won their love and respect through their children. I had known Doug and Robyn for several years as Vic and I went to the same home group mid week meeting with them for some time.

We held the wedding on the 18th June, 2005 in the courtyard at Peninsula Palms with the residents watching from their balconies which overlooked the courtyard. I walked down the aisle, or the path, with my granddaughter Lacey who was just five at the time. Doug's son Trevor and my son Jamie were witnesses and Pastor Earle Tongs performed the wedding. We had soup and dessert at Gai and Nev Turner's house after the wedding. It was very nice. We went to Landsborough for a couple of nights for our honeymoon. Matt didn't attend the wedding because Phionna was going to be there. But Jamie and Robert, and my nephew Nathan, and my Mum and Dad were there. Also, Vic's brother John and his wife, and Vic's sister Vacelia and her husband came as well. Vic's children didn't attend. Doug's son Trevor was about to leave and work on the Operation Mobilisation (OM) ship as a chef, so we decided to get married before he went away.

We settled in my little house at Deception Bay until Doug sold his home at Clontarf and I sold my house. We then bought a house together just up the road from my house at Deception Bay. I became involved in my music, work and church. Doug worked in the kitchen at Peninsula Palms until he retired a couple of years later.

We have done some interesting things over the years. We went to the UK and to Paris after we moved into the house we bought. Doug had been born in Halifax, near Hebden Bridge, where his family lived in Yorkshire and came to Australia with his parents and brother when he was just nine. He'd never been back and so we had had a month away. Our plane had been delayed in Brisbane for a night and so we arrived in London later than planned. We then caught the Euro Star train to Paris and we had two nights there. What an experience seeing the Eiffel Tower and the Louvre Museum. It was great, we went back to London and hired a car and drove to Poole in the south of England and stayed for a couple of days with some friends of Doug's. We then drove up to Hebden Bridge and stayed in the White Lion Hotel. Doug's parents had their honeymoon at that hotel. Doug's father's cousin and his wife still lived there so we spent time with them. We also attended the local Church of England where Doug's parents had married. There was an old lady there who remembered Doug's parents. She thought Doug looked very much like his father.

We then drove up to the Lakes District before driving to meet the ferry to go over to Ireland. We left the hire car there and picked up another one when we arrived in Ireland. We stayed in Dublin at a huge house run by the missionary organization, Ireland Outreach. The property was called "Charleville" which has since been sold. We stayed there for a week and just did day trips to different places in Ireland. We didn't get up to Northern Ireland, but enjoyed the places that we did see. We then flew out from Dublin to fly directly home. It was a wonderful experience. Doug enjoyed going back to where he had spent his early childhood. He had many memories of his time there and his little town was almost unchanged from all those years ago.

We did our first cruise to New Caledonia, Venuatu and Lifour Island. This was a great experience and we met up with another two couples that we knew which made it more interesting. We disembarked at Noumea in New Caledonia and did a bus tour, also at Vanuatu and Lifour Island. We didn't get the cruising bug like the people we met up with, but we enjoyed it just the same.

We also toured New Zealand and drove up to the North island and stayed with Doug's cousin Heather and her husband Phillip. We saw lots of beautiful scenery, it is a beautiful country.

We also hired a car and travelled around Tasmania. This was a great trip too. We stayed with some friends of Doug's and just did day trips from their place for three days.

During our marriage we became involved with a ministry organization called Trans World Radio (TWR) and Project Hannah with Charles and Val Gray. We were involved with them doing church visitation for several years. Val and I had a Project Hannah prayer group for several years as well. Then Val and Charles retired as they became older, we didn't want to take it on so we retired from the ministry as well.

This ministry uses the big short wave broadcast radios to reach many countries where Christianity is banned. Project Hannah is a ministry of the prevention and rehabilitation of survivors of human trafficking, especially women and girls.

They could hear the gospel over the little solar powered radios that this ministry was able to give out to many people in those closed countries. I wrote this song from the perspective of a girl caught up and trafficked in one of those countries.

Song for Hannah

1. I was born a girl in a poor man's world
Too many mouths to feed
So they took me away 'cause nobody cared.
They said they'd come and get me
when they could afford to feed me
I cried out and asked "is anybody there"?
(Chorus)
"Who's gonna come and get me and help to ease my pain
Who's gonna come and save me, I'm cryin' out in vain"?

2. Too many men have come and gone,
Too many promises have come undone
My childhood's gone, no wedding vows
My tears they fall like raindrops, nobody seems to care
I cry out and ask "Is anybody there".

(Chorus 2)
3. Then someone turned the radio on,
I couldn't believe my ears
There was somebody out there who really cares

They said His Name was Jesus and He died for all my sin
I cried out and there was somebody there.

(Chorus 3)
Jesus would come and save me and take away my shame
They said he really loves me and my cryin's not in vain.

4. So I gave my heart to Jesus and He helped to ease my pain
I know He really loves me and He took away my shame.
My Jesus really loves me and my cryings not in vain.

Church Ministry

I became involved with the Mueller Ladies' Ministry Breakfast Club. Pauline Robins first came up with the idea for a breakfast for women and some spiritual encouragement. After some years we met meet in the managers home at Peninsula Palms Retirement Village. The manager's wife Alice, did all the cooking for the breakfasts which we held once a month. She did the cooking for the breakfasts until Alice and her husband bought a house at Deception Bay where she began doing the cooking for it at the new house. We raised money and supported a young person through the ministry of Transform the Nations.

The breakfasts then moved to Mueller Community Church and have been doing so for the past several years. We originally asked ladies to do the breakfast each month until Covid 19 hit and we had to change the way of doing food. The committee had to do a TAFE course for dining in and we weren't able to cook at home and bring it in. This was a challenge as we had to have individually wrapped food or have a caterer bring food in which is more expensive. This ministry is still going strong and a number of ladies from the

Retirement Village always attend. I decided to retire from the committee at the end of 2021. My roles on the committee have been treasurer, catering, Facebook page, and a monthly newsletter.

I had also been leading a Know Your Bible (KYB) Bible study group for several years at Mueller. This is a ministry of Christian Women Communicating International (CWCI). I was involved in the CWCI Safari Ministry for 20 years and resigned from it in 2019. It was such a privilege to share the Word of God with the ladies. Each term we would study either a book from the New Testament or alternatively a book from the Old Testament or a topical subject. I have learned so much about God and His Word through this ministry.

Christian Women Communicating International (CWCI)

CWCI stands for Christian Women Communicating International – a worldwide Bible-based faith ministry that had its in beginnings in Australia in 1957.

Initiated by Grace Collins, Bible-teaching Events for women have been hosted by committees in capital cities and regional areas across Australia since 1957. Since 1971 Safari teams have taken events into rural and remote areas. Events and Safaris offer encouraging, inspiring, biblical teaching for women, bringing women to a personal knowledge of Jesus Christ as Saviour and equipping them for life in their homes, work, and communities.

Know Your Bible (KYB) is CWCI's most well-known ministry. KYB founder, Jean Raddon, commenced production of these carefully designed Bible studies in 1972. Available for use in face2face or online groups or by correspondence, KYB studies are in use across Australia, Melanesia and overseas. They are also made available for non-CWCI study groups via our Head Office in Sydney. In all these ways, together with our website [cwciaus.org.au], Blog and social media posts, Bond newsletter and other publications CWCI Australia ministries aim to grow women in Christ through sharing the Bible. (cwciaus.org.au)

The Safaris' ministry involved two or three women going out into the country in a car and sometimes a small plane, to minister to the ladies in the country in more isolated areas. I was the leader, singer, driver and only missed two safaris over the years I was involved. I saw so much of the country that I wouldn't otherwise have seen. What a wonderful experience! I went with a number of speakers from CWCI, a different one on each safari, each one had their own way of sharing from the Bible and I learned a lot from those lovely ladies. The highlight was in 2017 when I did a National Safari from Broken Hill in a small plane which was piloted by the "Flying Padre" from the Uniting Church Flying patrol. I went with another lady, Anne, who was the speaker and we flew from Broken Hill to a number of small towns in NSW, up to Thargominda in Qld, then down to Mildura in Victoria. We even flew to my home town of Griffith. What a joy it was to hold a meeting there, and my sister Leonie was able to attend. It was sad to have to give it all up but I have many happy memories of my time with CWCI and meeting so many beautiful country folk. It was during this trip that my mother and my sister Leonie, informed me of my brother's terminal illness.

Doug and I were also involved with the Country Gospel Music Club Brisbane. I was Vice-President and then President. I played and sang and eventually played keyboard in the Good News Country Band. Doug was the sound man for several years until his memory started troubling him and it became too hard. Due to Covid 19 we eventually closed the club down as it was too hard with all the rules and regulations. But we had many happy times there.,

Doug and I were members of an antique car club and had many outings with the group going on car rallies. Doug had an old Rover car which we took on these rallies. We made friends with a couple of local couples which we still see from time to time. Doug resigned from the club in 2021, because he was no longer able to drive due to his mild cognitive impairment.

We bought an old caravan a few years ago and we had taken it a few times on holiday and each year to the Nanango Country Muster, which we both enjoyed. We haven't been to the muster for a couple of years due to the Covid 19 lock downs. The van came in handy as a spare bedroom, but we eventually sold it as with Doug unable to drive, it was time to get rid of it.

My little dog Taffy died at age sixteen, which was sad. We also had Doug's little dog Timmy and he lived until seventeen! We then found Cassie, a beautiful black cocker spaniel at the local animal refuge. She was just four and had been found wandering. She and I bonded straight away and she loved me. She passed away at age fifteen. It was very sad and so hard to leave a pet that you've had for so long.

I had two beautiful cats, Cleo and Cuddles which I'd been given after Vic died. They were sisters and I loved those girls so much. They lived until they were eighteen! They died just a few months apart. I still miss my beautiful cats and my little dog.

We had Nelson the Cocker Spaniel to look after for a friend. He went to live with Trevor when we moved into the retirement village in April 2024. We now have Minni the Manx cat, and Penny, a beautiful tortoiseshell moggie. She's Doug's cat and Minni is mine.

With Ethel on safari

Rose and Doug

Chapter 18

AXESS RECORDING STUDIO

> *It is good to give thanks to the Lord, to sing praises to the Most High. It is good to proclaim your unfailing love in the morning, Your faithfulness in the evening, accompanied by a ten-stringed instrument, a harp, and the melody of a lyre. You thrill me, Lord, with all you have done for me! I sing for joy because of what You have done. Psalm 92: 1-3 (NLT)*
> *I put this Psalm to music, adapted from Psalm 92.*

Before Vic passed away, he asked his brother John Sophios, who has a home recording studio, whether he would record some of mine and Vic's original songs.

So, in 2004, we began recording my first album featuring my country gospel songs, Vic's songs and a couple that we wrote together. It is called He Set The Captives Free, which is also the title of one of Vic's songs. It was a great experience working with John and I really got to know him during the process. John played bass guitar, lead guitar, programming drums and some harmonies. His friend Dooley, who also used to be in Vic's band with John many years ago, played the piano beautifully on it as well. John did this recording for nothing in memory of his brother. Another one of John's friends played lead guitar on my last album.

He Set The Captives Free

1. There was Man from Galilee, He touched the blind so they could see
And His name was Jesus
He healed the sick, the lame could walk, He
touched the dumb so they could talk
Jesus came and He heard their call, and he healed them all.

Well he died upon that tree, just for you and me
It was on Calvary, O why can't they see
That He died upon that tree, to set the captive free.

2. Well a little girl, she up and died, it was so sad the whole town cried
Then Jesus came
He told the little girl to rise, then she opened up her eyes
The word of God from the King, death O where's your sting. (Chorus)

3. Then they came, took Him away, He had nothing more to say
And Jesus suffered
And through the trial and tribulation, all the pain and confrontation
They crucified Him on that hill, prophecy fulfilled. (Chorus)

4. Then the Age of Grace was born, the moment that the veil was torn
And Jesus died
Three days later He arose, that's the way the story goes
He's the one that we adore, He's alive forevermore. (Chrous).
Written by Victor James Sophios
(From Rose's Album "He Set the Captives Free (Copyright 2004).

Then a couple of years later, we recorded another country gospel album with more of mine and Vic's songs. This was called Open Up Your Heart. I'd made enough from sales from the first CD to pay for this album. My friend, Liz West, played her mandolin accompanying me in a couple of songs and also sang harmony. Again, John played bass, lead, drums, some harmony and his friend Dooley played piano again and also sang harmony.

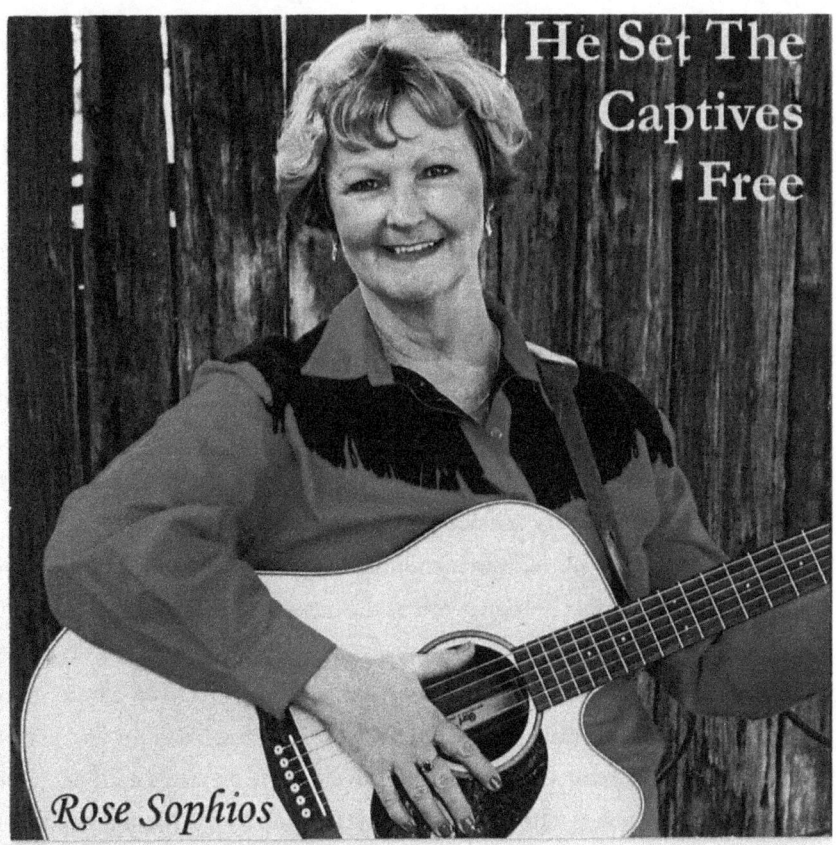

Rose Sophios with guitar *He Set The Captives Free* CD

Chapter 19

West'n Rose

> *Where is God my Creator, the One who gives*
> *songs in the night. Job 35:10 (NLT)*

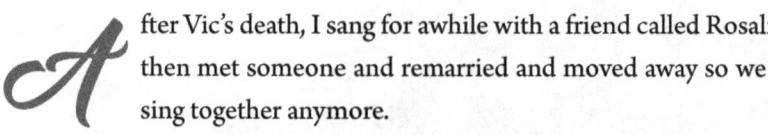fter Vic's death, I sang for awhile with a friend called Rosalie. She then met someone and remarried and moved away so we didn't sing together anymore.

I had met another friend, Liz West, and Liz sang and played guitar, piano, and mandolin. We found that our voices blended well and that Liz was a natural alto, and she was very musical too. So began our duo as West'n Rose. I played guitar and Liz played the mandolin. We were asked to perform at the Country Gospel Music Club each year as the guest artists, and also at different churches.

After recording my first two albums, Liz and I recorded an album of all my original songs. We called it "Life's Highway." Liz sang harmony and played mandolin on this album. One of the songs that I wrote on it was entitled, "God My Maker, Gives Songs in the Night", taken from Job 35:10. Most of the songs that I have written came about during the night. We sang together right up until Covid 19 closed things down and I retired from singing, so we folded our West'n Rose duo sadly. We had a lot of fun singing together.

The highlight of our time together was when Liz and I travelled to Tamworth for the Country Music Festival and sang in the country gospel tent. This festival is held every year in January. One of the churches in Tamworth always put on a country gospel event for country gospel music with a number of guest artists, and we were invited to appear. Other memories are the tribute night for our friend, John Hockey, who had passed away suddenly. We also sang at an aged care facility in Caloundra and it was very special when the residents in the dementia ward were singing along with us. We sang every year at different aged care facilities singing Christmas carols and songs, and also Australia Day concerts.

I won a prize in Canada for the best Country Gospel CD, "Open up Your Heart", but I had to go to Canada to receive it, and unfortunately I wasn't able to all the way to Canada, due to the expense.

I wrote this song about my life travelling on Life's Highway which eventually led me to the saving Grace of the Lord Jesus Christ. This is the title of the album that Liz and I recorded as West'n Rose.

Open Up Your Heart CD

Life's Highway

1. If I didn't have the Lord to show me the way
I'd be lost and afraid along life's highway
If I didn't have Jesus to heal all my pain
I'd be sick and hurting, trying to hide my pain.

(Chorus) If the Lord wasn't with me each hour of the day
I'd be lost and lonely, trying to find the way
If I didn't have the Lord to show me the way
I'd be lost and afraid along life's highway.

2. If He didn't give me His strength and His love
I'd be weak and tormented without help from above
If I didn't have Jesus just to get me through
O Lord, I couldn't get through life without you. (Chorus)

Bridge:-
My life had no meaning 'til He came along
O how could I help to not sing Him a song
Now that I have Jesus to show me the way
I'm no longer lost along life's highway.
(Chorus)
Now the Lord is with me each hour of the day
I'm no longer lonely, trying to find the way
Now that I have Jesus to show me the way
I'm no longer lost along Life's highway.
I'm no longer lost along life's highway

Life's Highway CD

Riverina Girl CD

Chapter 20

Riverina Girl

> *O sing to the Lord a new song, For He has done*
> *marvellous things, Shout joyfully to the Lord all the earth,*
> *Break forth into song, rejoice and sing. Psalm 98:1, 4-6*
> *I wrote a song and put the music to*
> *it adapted from this Psalm.*

My last album that I recorded with John, was Riverina Girl. This was some traditional original songs that I had written about my life in the Riverina, and some country gospel songs. I had also found 3 songs that Vic had written but I'd never heard him sing them, so I put the music to them and we put them on the album.

Again, John played bass, lead, drums and some harmony and Dooley again played piano and some harmony. Also, another one of John's friends Daryl, played lead guitar on two songs. The reason for the title is because I grew up in the Riverina and I will always be a Riverina Girl.

Riverina Girl

Written by Rose

I grew up in the Western Riverina
Not far from where the Murrumbidgee flows
Where golden wattle paints a pretty picture
And the purple Riverina blue bell grows.

(Chorus) I'm still a Riverina Girl, living in a city world
Longing to go back where my heart yearns
To where the Murrumbidgee flows
And the River Gums they grow
This Riverina Girl longs to return.

Where the magpie warbles out its pretty tune
And the kookaburra laughs from tall gum trees
My mind goes back to days when I was young
And the golden wattles blowing in the breeze. (Chorus)

As I reminisce about those days gone by
Swimming where the Murrumbidgee flows
Christmases and bonfires on the farm
Those memories, they seem so long ago. (Chorus)

After Covid 19, I found that my voice had weakened and I couldn't sing so well anymore. I don't sing solo much anymore, but still play guitar in the church worship team and the ukelele group that I've now joined at the retirement village. This is a lot of fun.

History of the Murrumbidgee Irrigation Area in the Riverina

The Murrumbidgee Irrigation Area (MIA) is geographically located within the Riverina area of New South Wales. It was created to control and divert the flow of local river and creek systems for the purpose of food production. The main river systems feeding and fed by the area are the Murrumbidgee and the Tumut. It is one of the most diverse and productive regions in Australia contributing over A$5 billion annually to the Australian economy.

As a result of the New South Wales Royal Commission into the Conservation of Water in the 1880s, the establishment of the MIA commenced in 1903 with the construction of canals west of Narrandera and the construction of Burrinjuck Dam.

The MIA was formally established in 1912 after the commissioning of the Burrinjuck Dam on the Murrumbidgee River. Further expansion occurred in the 1970s with the completion of the Snowy Mountains Scheme and construction of Blowering Dam on the Tumut River, which meets the Murrumbidgee near Gundagai. Subsequent expansion of Burrinjuck Dam led to further expansion of the MIA and as well as the capacity to generate hydro-electricity.

The system is still regarded as a major engineering achievement comprising an elaborate series of weirs, canals and holding ponds (fed by upstream rivers and dams).

Many of the towns within the area which include Leeton and Griffith were purpose built and designed for the project and remain as thriving communities today. The two towns are growing at a rapid rate due to sustainable employment. The growth of inland centres is unusual for central New South Wales which displays the uniqueness of the MIA.

The layout of the towns of Griffith and Leeton were designed in 1914 by Walter Burley Griffin, an American architect and town planner who had just won the competition for the plan for Canberra in 1912. (Source: www.wikipedia.org)

Chapter 21

Rose's Family

> *God decided in advance to adopt us into His own family by bringing us to himself through Jesus Christ. This is what He wanted to do, and it gave Him great pleasure. Ephesians 1:5 (NLT)*

My youngest sister, Leonie, still lives in Griffith with her husband Greg Walton. Their children both live in Melbourne with their families. I try to get down to Griffith once a year when I can. I enjoy going back there to see Leonie and Greg, some cousins and old school friends. I always visit the cemetery to check on Belinda's grave, and other relatives graves too. For years I didn't like going back to Griffith as there were too many bad memories there. But I seem to have dealt with that over the years and I now enjoy going back.

Jamie and Megan live in Morayfield and they have guinea pigs and ducks. Megan has recently spent most of 2024 going through breast cancer treatment. She had a lump out of her breast and had sixteen rounds of chemotherapy and then four weeks of radiation therapy. She has come through it and is now doing well. Jamie finally left Suncorp where he'd worked for many years, and is now with QANTAS working from home. (They have been together for over 20 years.)

Matthew has 4 children. Bailey, Lacey-Jane, Evi and Isla. Matt now lives on his own at Canungra. Robert, born in 1981, lives at Margate in a Department of Housing unit and is not far from Doug and I. He's doing okay and has NDIS support. He comes over to us often and comes to church with us. I have a lot to do with him and often take him to his appointments. He accepted Jesus Christ as his Saviour in his teens. He's a gentle soul and he and I have a very close bond, as does he and Jamie. Robert had moved out of home and had a small flat at Strathpine after Vic's death. Then he was able to get into the Department of Housing and found a unit at Nundah, about 40 minutes away from me. He was with a government agency called Youth Care and it was that organization that found him the unit at Nundah. He lived there for until August 2018 when he finally got a transfer over to Margate which is much closer to me. He has settled in there well and has a small unit. His mental illness is stable and he keeps on his medication.

Robert has a very good National Disability Insurance Scheme (NDIS) plan. He now has a support worker who takes him shopping. Another support worker helps Rob with his housework. Another one takes him for a drive, a movie, or swimming at the local heated pool, a walk along the beach, or they go to the library. They will often go for a drive around the Redcliffe Peninsula to make up the 2 hours allocated to Robert. Robert is getting better out in public but doesn't like crowds as he suffers from anxiety. He has improved over the years and is managing his mental illness with support and of course good medication.

My sister, Esther

My beautiful sister Esther, passed away on the 6th September, 2021 from Motor Neurone Disease (MND). This is a terrible disease. I was able to see her a couple of weeks before she passed away. But in March 2021, Robert and I went up to see her and I was able to lead her to the saving grace of the Lord Jesus Christ. She could no longer speak but would write on paper what she wanted to say. She was ready, and she knew where she was going when she died.

Believe in the Lord Jesus and you will be saved. Acts 16:31

She planned her own funeral and it was very God-honouring. It was a lovely graveside service. She chose two beautiful hymns that were played and sung by Elvis Presley. "In The Garden", and "Who Am I". So appropriate. Our state was in Covid lockdown, so only Queenslanders were able to attend. My sister, Leonie, and her husband were unable to come from Griffith in New South Wales. But Esther's daughter Renee recorded it and put it on Facebook, so they were able to watch it. Esther leaves behind four children, Rebecca, Leigh, Renee and Scott and five grandchildren.

Esther's eldest daughter, Rebecca lives in Brisbane, Leigh is married to Melissa and they have 3 sons. Renee is married to Scott who has 2 children and they live in Rockhampton. Esther's youngest son Scott has two children, whose mum is Alissa. Rebecca moved back to Yeppoon in 2020 to look after her mother, and she did this admirably. She has since moved back to Brisbane. Renee also looked after her mother and also looked after her grandmother, my mother! Those girls are very caring and also Leigh, who lives in Yeppoon, was a great support to his mother Esther and grandmother.

Esther was still married to her husband "Winkie" but they had been separated for many years, so he and his partner have moved into Esther's house as he was still half owner. Esther had looked after our mother for all the years Mum lived in Yeppoon. She was very good to Mum and we appreciated all that she did for her. Esther loved her garden, and also crocheting. She did mending for other people and had a number of regular clients. Her crochet work is exceptional and we all have some of her beautiful work. She made Leonie and I a lovely tablecloth for our 70th birthdays. She finished Leonie's just in time. She had previously worked for a number of years at the local St Brendan's Boys College.

Esther loved country music and especially Elvis songs. She would often have her music playing while she was in the garden or doing her sewing. I don't think she ever recovered emotionally from her husband leaving her for her friend. She never found anyone else to share her life with and just lived for her kids, grand kids and our mother. She was a very kind and caring person. She is greatly missed by many people. Leonie and I are very grateful for her care for Mum when Mum moved up to Yeppoon. It was very sad to see her gradually lose her ability to speak, to eat and to walk. Motor Nuerone Disease is a cruel disease.

The Woman at the Well

Robert

Jamie, Rose & Matt

Chapter 22

Doug's Family

> *Praise the Lord! How joyful are those who fear the Lord and delight in obeying his commands. Their children will be successful everywhere; an entire generation of godly people will be blessed... and their good deeds will last forever. Psalm 112:1-3*

Doug's parents, Doug Snr and Irene, passed away several years ago and he has a sister Susan, who lives in Victoria with her husband Scott and four children. Doug's parents were "Ten Pound Poms" who came to Australia in the 1950s. Doug had a brother Stephan who was killed in his teens in a car accident. Doug's sister comes up periodically to see Doug and his family. We also called in to see them several times on our trips to Victoria to see Doug's daughter Sarah and her family when they lived in Melbourne.

Doug's daughter, Sarah, and her husband Sam and family moved to Melbourne in 2011 and so we made many a trip down there to see them, They would come up here every second year and we'd go down there on the other year. Doug would often go in winter, which I stopped doing as it was far too cold for me. They have now moved back to Qld and live in Brisbane. Both have jobs and their two sons are working and their daughter is at University.

Trudy and Michael and their three children live just outside Caboolture and the three boys are all now working. Michael is a fly in fly out worker on a mine site. Trudy is working in aged care and is now an Enrolled Nurse (EN).

Trevor lives out at Trudy's in the granny flat and has worked on a local strawberry farm since Covid 19, but he is now back at the local hotel that he used to work at, as a qualified chef. He comes over at least once a week and takes Doug out for a coffee and a drive. Trudy and Sarah also take him out or have him over for a night.

Some of the other holidays that Doug and I have had were up to Cairns and to Ravenshoe several times to visit my late brother Stan and his wife Jan. We did the Sky Rail and the old train down the mountain range to Cairns. We also made many trips to Melbourne to see Doug's daughter Sarah and her family. We made yearly trips together to Yeppoon to visit my Mum and my late sister Esther. I did several trips also on my own or once a year with Robert.

Another memorable holiday was to Tasmania where we flew down and hired a car and drove from the west side to the east side. We stayed a few nights with some of Doug's friends in Hobart. We visited a number of historical sights. Tasmania is a very interesting state.

In 2021, we finally went on a whale watching trip from Redcliffe. We've lived here all this time and had never been on the whale watch. It was spectacular and we saw many whales and a number of pods which put on a good show for us. Trevor gave us this trip for Doug's 75th birthday. It was well worth it.

For the past several years, Doug's memory has been declining. He was firstly diagnosed with Mild Cognitive Impairment several years ago, then in 2021 he was diagnosed with early dementia. His short-term memory is getting worse, but his long-term memory is still quite good. There are many things that he is unable to do anymore, one being driving. The doctor would not sign off his medical when he was due to have his license renewed at age 75. This was pretty hard for him as his life has been around cars. He loves old cars and sold his English "Rover" a couple of years ago. Just recently he gave his Holden away. So we are now a one car family!

He finds technical things very hard now and can't grasp some of the things he could do easily. I am now looking after the finances as he can't handle money anymore. For someone who was once the paymaster for the Baptist Union of Queensland, that's very difficult for him and he gets frustrated with not being able to remember. I am trying to be supportive and also find it frustrating, as I also have Robert with his mental illness and I am always reminding him of his appointments and to do daily chores.

I attend a support group meeting each month, for the mentally ill. This also gives me some perspective on Doug's condition which is like a mental illness.

Chapter 23

NEW CHURCH UPDATE 2022

> *He makes the whole body fit together perfectly. As each part does its own special work, it helps the other parts grow, so that the whole body is healthy and growing and full of love. Ephesians 4:16 (NLT)*

*I*n late 2021, Doug and I made the decision to leave Mueller Community Church. The main focus of this church was the school, Mueller College, and this is understandable as it's a real mission field right there. For Doug and Robert who preferred a smaller church, we made the move to Deception Bay Baptist Church which is not far from where we live. I felt it was time to have a new focus as I was finding the things I used to enjoy at Mueller, I wasn't enjoying anymore. So over the last 12 months I have gradually dropped doing a lot of the activities that I was involved in. I am no longer on the Breakfast Club Committee, have handed my KYB group over to another very capable lady, my good friend Dr Pam Harvey. I had been taken off the music team just after church resumed after the first Covid 19 wave. I finalised doing the Breakfast Club newsletter at the end of the year of 2022.

At D Bay Baptist, I am playing guitar in the worship team most Sundays. I am involved in the womens' ministry with my friend Lorna. I have joined a

KYB group at the church as a participant and not a leader. Robert comes over every second Saturday and stays the night to come to church with me Sunday morning. I have to go a bit earlier for music practice, so he and Doug have to come with me. It's nice to not have so much responsibility and I can relax and enjoy church more.

We have a ladies' activity each month at our church and each one has been well attended. Lorna and I work well together. She's the planner and I do a lot of the computer work, newsletters etc.

Foot Surgery

Early November of 2022 I had foot surgery to fix some arthritis trouble spots on my right foot. Also a bone fusion and the surgeon has also fixed the bunion surgery I had several years ago. This went extremely well and my foot has healed well. No more pain!

I had been going to the PCYC gym and senior's exercise class for a number of years. I had an MRI on my spine due to back pain in 2023 and the findings were not good. I have a lot of arthritis in most of my vertebrae so have been going to a physio also. This has helped me a lot and I very rarely have to take pain killers. Some days I have pain but it is manageable. Exercise is definitely helping. I go to an exercise physiologist who helps me with exercise.

My thumbs are giving me problems now from severe osteoarthritis in my hands. I have a trigger finger on both hands, same finger! This can be very painful so have had to give my patchwork sewing a rest for awhile. I love sewing and patchwork especially. I make a number of quilts each year for our stalls held twice a year, to raise money for school chaplains and our own church youth group. I'm dreading having to give up playing the guitar or piano, but so far I can manage okay. I will be seeing a hand surgeon early in 2025.

One health issue that has plagued me all of my adult life is migraine headaches. I've suffered from them for as long as I can remember. I was told that once you have passed menopause, they'll be a thing of the past! Sorry, they were wrong! I now have good medication to take when I feel one coming on. Sometimes I can go for weeks and not have one, then I can have as many as four or five in a row, mostly coming on in the early hours of the morning.

Early in 2024 I had a profound feeling that this would be the year that we sell our house and move into a retirement village. We put the house on the market in February and had it sold within six days! We had twelve offers and the amount we ended up getting was quite astounding! We then had a villa available at The Village Retirement Village in Rothwell. At first it was not available for six months, but within a week we were offered a villa and had moved in 10th April, 2024.

Doug's family and our friend Steve helped us pack up and move. We had to severely down size to a 3 bedroom duplex villa. We gave away a lot of our stuff and I bought some new furniture. It's a lovely unit and quite spacious. We have a room each and a spare room that has a bed and is also my sewing room. I gave most of my musical equipment to Doug's granddaughter Clem, as she is quite musical and I gave my bass guitar to Miles. I now have one acoustic guitar, a keyboard and a ukelele.

Chapter 24

My Mum

Honour your father and mother, so that you may live long in the land then Lord your God is giving you. Exodus 20:12

Mum moved up to Yeppoon in 2008 and she moved into the Capricorn Adventist Retirement Village. She had a lovely 1 bedroom duplex. She soon became involved in the activities of the village and made a number of new friends. She became involved in her church group up there and she still and her little car. She had some issues with her hip after being there for a number of years otherwise she kept good health.

Mum's two brothers passed away a number of years ago, then her dear sister Ruth also passed away several years ago. They were especially close as sisters. So there was just Mum and her youngest sister Margaret left.

Mum turned 90 years old in 2014 and Esther, Leonie and I helped organise a 90th birthday party for her. My brother Stan, and his wife Jan, came from their home in Ravenshoe, on the Atherton tablelands. Leonie and Greg drove up from Griffith, Doug, Robert and my granddaughter Lacey-Jane and myself drove up from our home in Deception Bay. Dad's brother John (since passed away) from Wagga flew up with Auntie Margie from Canberra. Uncle John's wife Ruth, had passed away by then. A number of my cousins also came up for the occasion. We had the party at Esther's house. All of her kids were also there. My niece, Aimee, also came up with her family.

Esther's family who live in Yeppoon. My son, Jamie, drove up. Matt wasn't able to come. Many of Mum's church friends and some of our other relatives were also there. It was wonderful celebration of Mum's long life. It was great that her four children were all still around to celebrate with her. She finally had a hip replacement the following year and did very well. Esther and I were with her to support her after her operation. She did well and just used a wheelie walker after that. She's also had a pacemaker put in earlier to regulate her heart. So she survived another almost nine years after that!

Mum passed away in 2023 aged ninety nine, at the Capricorn Adventist Nursing Home Yeppoon. She was in independent living and we have her name down for a place in the care facility as she was starting to decline in her health. She was only in there for a few months until she passed away 27th August 2023. She still had a sharp mind which was a wonderful thing at her age. I had been driving up to Yeppoon several times a year to see her as she started to decline in her health. Leonie and Greg would come up at least once a year, sometimes more, when they were able.

I had been up six times during 2023 as I was concerned for her. My sister Leonie and her husband Greg had also been up a couple of times that year. We are very grateful to our niece Renee who looked after all Mum's finances etc and looked in in her most days. She's a very loving and caring granddaughter. My niece Rebecca also came up when it looked like Mum was fading and so Leonie, Renee, Rebecca and I were all with Mum as she passed away.

Mum had planned and paid for her funeral and so all we had to do was to put it in place. She didn't want a eulogy so I prepared something to say as a thank you to Mum's family and friends. Leonie read out a lovely poem that Renee had given us that Mum had given her to be read out at Esther's funeral.

A number of Mum's grandchildren came up for the funeral. Stan's widow Jan and her brother Archie came as did many of Mum's church friends. Her two special friends Joan and Cheryl were very close to Mum and were able to say goodbye to her the day before she passed away. There were staff members from CARV the care facility as well. Mum was very much loved and respected. Two of the preachers from her church did the service. We sang two hymns that Mum had picked.

It was a relief in a way that Mum had now gone, but sad as she will be so missed. Leonie and I designed the plaque for her grave where she's buried in with Esther.

MUM'S GRAVESIDE SERVICE- YEPPOON CEMETERY

Elizabeth Jane Haworth- 26/6/1924- 27/8/2023

MY TRIBUTE BY ROSE

Mum didn't want to have a eulogy so....

On behalf of myself and husband Doug, my children and Doug's children, my sister Leonie and her husband Greg, and their children, Mum's sister our Auntie Margie in Canberra, and all of Mums grandchildren and great grandchildren, we thank you for coming today to say farewell to our mother, sister, grandmother, Auntie.

We'd like to take this opportunity to thank a few people who have stood in the gap for me and Leonie when we couldn't be here, due to our living in other parts of the country.

Firstly, Renee and Beccy, Mum's grandaughters who cared for their own mother until her passing. Then Beccy went back to Brisbane, Renee then took up the responsibility of caring for our mother. Renee, you have a God Given gift of caring and all of Mum's family thank you for looking after your Nan, your grandmother, our mother. Leonie and I appreciate every thing that you did for Mum. You showed her love, care and compassion and we say thank you. Thank you for helping out with the funeral arrangements. Renee designed the bookmarks and had them printed as well as the hymn sheet.

For Cheryl and Joan, Mum's friends. We appreciate all that you have done for Mum, and we say thank you. You have been wonderful friends to our mother, your friend. You treated her as if she were your own mother.

For CARV independent living and the the care facility, we say thank you to you and your carers for looking after our mother.

To Mum's neighbours, Colin, Kevin, Merv and all the ladies, two of whom are here today along with Colin. Mum looked forward to Happy Hour at 4 pm each day, even when she wasn't well, she loved to go out and listen to you all chatting and sharing lollies.

So from Leonie and Greg, Sharon, Nigel and Trish and children, Myself and Doug, Jamie and Megan, Matt and his 4 children, and their mums' Charli and Phionna, and my son Robert. From Stans children, Nathan and Chrissie and children, Aimee and Greg and children,

Tammie and Zane. Aiden and Hosanna and children, Esthers children, Rebecca, Leigh and Melissa and boys, Renee and Scott and Blake, Scotty and his children, Auntie Margie and her family in Canberra, John and Robyn Stan's widow Jan and her brother Archie. From my cousins, Ron, Dianne, Jill and Jim and their partners and family and all of our cousins.

And all of those whose lives have been touched by Mum's love, thank you for caring about our mother, and thank you for honouring her today.

Thank you to the grandchildren who have flown a long way to be here today.

John 14:1-3 says, "Do not let your hearts be troubled, You believe in God; believe also in Me. My Father's house has many rooms; if it were not so, would I have told you that I am going there to prepare a place for you? And if I go and prepare a place for you, I will come back and take you to be with me that you also may be where I am.

Leonie and I went through Mum's papers and we found this one which we'd like to read today. Mum kept everything. Leonie will read it.

Read "God Knows Your Days" - Read by Leonie

> God knows our days-the days of darkest sorrow
> When crushing grief hath stunned the heart with pain
> When no desire seems left that life tomorrow

Should pleasant be, or smile, or shine again.
He knows our days of overwhelming weakness
When laid aside we may not join the throng
Knows to the days when-all through Christ's own
     meekness
We silent suffer insult shame or wrong
He knows the days when conflict strong is raging
When wicked hosts our spirits sore assail
He knows the warfare we through Christ are
     waging
Knows to, and waits to lift us when we fall
He knows our days, the darkest and the brightest
He knows each day He knows them one and all.

One thing we'll always remember is Mum's beautiful smile

Order of service

Chris, the Preacher from Mum's church, opened with a
     little about Mum
1st hymn -- Nearer Still Nearer, Close to Thine heart

Rose and Leonie shared the above.
Renee shared and read a poem, on the back of the book
     mark- Esther's daughter
Tammie shared memories of her Nan, teaching her to
     make scones and the holidays they had with Nan
     and Grandad - Stan's daughter

Nathan shared memories of his Nan out on the farm - Stan's son

Jamie shared memories of his Nan out on the farm, how Nan taught him how to make chocolate mousse - Rose's son

Preacher Chris gave a message - Psalm 18 v 28 and also on the proverbs 31, the virtuous women.

Closing hymn - Abide with Me.

5 grandsons and one great grandson carried the coffin to the grave

Jamie, Nathan, Leigh, Leighs son Flynn, Scotty and Aiden.

Brady (Chris's offsider) closed in prayer.

The wake was at the local Sailing Club. Great time catching up with relies from all over the place. Alan and Anne Currie and their daughter Jodie and partner came.

It was a great time of story telling and reminiscing.

Auntie Margie

At Auntie Margie's wedding, sometime in the 1950s, I was probably about six, I think. The four of the girls who were our Auntie's flower girls, all had our hair curled for the occasion, but our cousin Ronnie, didn't like his sister Dianne's hair curly, so he went and put her under the tap and washed it out! That's why she had straight hair and the other three of us had curly hair!

Mum's last sibling, Margaret, is still with us and lives in Canberra. She has her son John, and daughter Robyn living nearby. She was the youngest in Mum's family and is now in her late 80's. Leonie and I went on a road trip in

March 2024 and we called in to see her at Canberra and had a couple of days there. We also had a night in Wagga Wagga to see Mum's sister-in-law, Win. Auntie Win was Dad's brother Jim's widow and she lives in a care facility there. She was a wealth of family information! We had a lovely time with her. We also caught up with one of her sons, David and his wife.

Aunt Margie's Wedding to Chris Phillips

My Mum

Four of us at Mums 90th

Mum & Auntie Margie

Mum at 99 years old

Mum's Plaque

Chapter 25

MY FRIEND ETHEL

> *The heartfelt counsel of a friend as as sweet as*
> *perfume and incense. Proverbs 27:9 (NLT)*

For 27 years, I have had a very special friend, Ethel. We first met when my late husband Vic and I lived at Petrie. Ethel and her husband John also lived there and we met up at Redcliffe Christian Assembly (now Mueller Community Church). Ethel was a speaker with Christian Women's Communicating International (CWCI). Eventually I became a singer, leader, driver for the ministry of CWCI ministering to women in the country and isolated towns in Australia, called Safaris. Ethel and I did two safaris together. We had some wonderful times together and met some amazing country ladies. Recently, Ethel has been diagnosed with dementia and her memory is slowly declining. Her husband John organised an 80th birthday for her and my friend Heather and I helped him put it together. This is what I shared about her at her birthday.

Ethel's 80th

I've known Ethel for 27 years. We first met when I was married to my late husband Vic. We were attending Mueller Church then known as RCA. We discovered that we both lived at Petrie, just a few streets away from each other. We soon became firm friends. Her and John were over at our place for a meal one evening. John and Ethel went off home after dinner as it was within walking distance. I thought Taffy had gone to bed, but I couldn't find him the next morning. So I rang Ethel to see if he was over at her place. She didn't think so, but they went outside to have a look and who should be under their car, but Taffy! He'd spent the night there!

Ethel was a speaker for CWCI and I started with the CWCI Safaris in 2001. My first safari was with Ethel and another lady, Yvonne. We went to the Central Highlands and Coal fields. One memorable time was when we stayed with a couple in Mt Morgan. There were 3 of us but only 2 beds. One was a double and one was a single on the verandah. So we decided, seeing as Ethel and I knew each other, we'd take the double bed, and Yvonne took the single. Well… there was much laughter and cackling that night as we thought it was quite a scream and chuckled about it for days.

Several years later we did another safari out to the Southern Border as far out as Charleville. This also included St George where John's late sister Ruth was living. It was lovely to see her at our meeting there. See my Safari album for some great photos.

But the funniest story of that trip was, we had left Cunnamulla, and we were to head to a little town called Bollan, on the way to St George. So we were chatting away and I'm the driver and we kept following the sign on the side of the road that said B and the milage. So driving on, lots of talking, until we came to a sign that said Welcome to NSW! We were following the sign to B for Bourke! I'd turned right instead of left back at the turn off to St George. So, we turned around and headed for B for Bollon, probably exceeding the speed limit as our meeting was for 10 am. No mobile phones, so couldn't ring the lady, just got to Bollon on an empty tank of fuel. Praise the Lord, the service station had just reopened two weeks before. So we filled up, got to the hall, and they hadn't started the meeting because a car load of ladies who were coming from another town, had a flat, and they were running late too. So it all ended well and we had a good meeting. So for several years, Ethel and I often laughed about B for Bollon!

Ethel and Vic organised my 50th birthday at her and John's house, and Vic passed away just five months later from stomach cancer. Doug and I were married 5 years after that, and Doug and Ethel organised my 60th birthday just after I'd had a knee replacement. I let her off for my 70th and I organised it myself! What a wonderful friend Ethel has been to me over the ups and downs of life. I have always tried to catch up with her every week over the past few years, unless we've both been away. Ethel prayed for me through many difficult situations in my life. You'll always be my "Bestie" Ethel. Happy 80th, and we'll continue to meet on Wednesdays and share lots of memories. God Bless. My best friend!

Rose, Ethel and Heather

Chapter 26

The Village Redcliffe

Retirement Community in Rothwell, Qld

But they that wait upon the Lord shall renew their strength; they shall mount up with wings as eagles; they shall run, and not be weary; and they shall walk, and not faint. Isaiah 40:31 (KJV)

We moved in on the 10th April, 2024. It's lovely village with 290 villas. It is one of 6 villages independently owned. There is a gym, 2 pools, 1 is heated and a Health and Wellness Centre where a number of activities are held. All allied health come there each week. Then there is the main community centre, coffee shop and admin, library, movie theatre. The coffee shop is open 5 days a week and they have breakfast, morning tea, and lunch. Special events are held there, entertainment, special morning teas etc. There is also a bowling green and small bowling club, a boulee and crochet court. The gardens are lovely and kept in good condition by a team of gardeners.

It's a secure village and the gates are closed at 4pm each day. We have a fob to get in if we're out after that time. Doug goes to a couple of the men's activities like men's morning tea, and men's sausage sizzle. There is a doctor who comes three times weekly, so I take Doug to him now.

I have joined a ukelele group which meets each Saturday afternoon. I also attend the ladies exercise class and the gym, also the heated pool. Water aerobics are on from late October through to Autumn when we do exercises in the Health and Wellness centre. It's very secure village and we have settled in well. Doug rides his motorised scooter around the village and outside, where he can ride to Bunnings which is nearby. I feel that it's a step toward the next step in case Doug may eventually need more care. We have enrolled with My Aged Care and are presently waiting to be approved for an Aged Care package.

I can now give thanks to God for my painful experiences, because I have been forgiven and set free from my past, and Jesus promised that He would never leave me or forsake me. He filled that emptiness in my heart and "His compassions are new every morning", and you can claim them daily.

> *The faithful love of the Lord never ends! His mercies never cease. Great is His faithfulness; His mercies begin afresh each morning. I say to myself, "The Lord is my inheritance; therefore, I will hope in Him!" Lamentations 3: 22-24 (NLT)*

Conclusions / Tributes / Epilogue

Thank you for allowing me to share my story with you. It's never too late to accept Jesus as your Lord and Saviour. It doesn't mean that that everything will immediately be okay. Jesus forgives us but the consequences of sin can still be there. But Jesus will help us through those consequences and help us to deal with them. He will never leave us when we put our trust in Him.

As I conclude my story I would like to pay tribute to the following who have had such a big influence in my life.

> **My Mum and Dad** never said "I told you so" after originally saying "you made your bed you lie in it", and always accepted me back and never judged me.
>
> **My brother Stan** who I still miss so much, loved me and we had a close bond.
>
> **My sister Esther** who always welcomed me at her place every time I went to visit her and Mum.
>
> **My late husband Vic** who helped me so much on my spiritual journey.
>
> **My sister Leonie** as we support each other now that our parents and Stan and Esther are gone.
>
> **My three best friends Ethel, Heather and Lorna**
>
> **Liz** with whom I enjoyed many happy years singing together.

> **Doug's family, Trevor, Trudy and Sarah** who are such a support to me and their father.
>
> **Doug** who accepted me warts and all!
>
> **My son Matthew** who gave me four beautiful grandchildren
>
> **My beautiful grandchildren** whom I love unconditionally and I know that they love me, and to their mothers **Phionna and Charli** who have always maintained contact with me.
>
> **Jamie, my eldest son,** has been my greatest support to me and also to Robert.
>
> **Megan** who has travelled a hard road recently.
>
> **My wonderful son Robert** who continues to struggle with life. I could not imagine my life without him.
>
> **Thank you to many friends** who have touched my life over the years.
>
> **The Lord Jesus Christ,** who loves me, who has forgiven me, and will never leave me or forsake me I know where I am going when my life on this earth is ended, to be with Him in heaven for eternity. I will see my darling daughter Belinda Jane for the first time as I know she's there in heaven.

Finally, a challenge - do you know that you can also have this assurance of heaven if you trust in Jesus Christ, God's Son, as your Lord and Saviour.

In the story of the Samaritan Woman in the Bible, Jesus knew all about her and yet He didn't judge her. The Samaritan heard the truth, received an eternal relationship with Jesus, then she became a missionary as she went back to her town and told others all about Jesus and what He had done for her. We are blind to our own need until Jesus opens our eyes. I was blind to my own need until Jesus met me where I was currently at. He forgave me my sin and my sinful lifestyle and He helped me by sending people into my life who were also able to help me to get my life back on track. I couldn't imagine my life without the Lord Jesus now.

Below are some Bible verses that are particularly special to me and I pray that they will encourage and inspire you too.

> Philippians 4:6-7 - "Do not be anxious about anything, but in everything by prayer and supplication with thanksgiving let your requests be made known to God. And the peace of God, which surpasses all understanding, will guard your hearts and your minds in Christ Jesus."
>
> 1 Thessalonians 5:18 - "Be thankful in all circumstances, for this is God's will for you who belong to Christ Jesus."
>
> Psalm 100:4 - "Enter His gates with thanksgiving and His courts with praise; give thanks to Him and praise His name."
>
> Colossians 2:6 - "So then, just as you received Christ Jesus as Lord, continue to live in Him, strengthened in their faith as you were taught, and overflowing with thankfulness."
>
> Isaiah 41:10 - "Fear not, for I am with you; be not dismayed, for I am your God; I will strengthen you, I will help you, I will uphold you with my righteous right hand."

God Bless,
Rose

Rose's CD's available for purchase:

He Set the Captives Free -Rose Sophios 2004
Open Up Your Heart- Rose Alexander 2007
Song for Hannah (single) 2008
Life's Highway- West'n Rose 2009
Riverina Girl - Rose Alexander 2012

All albums © Rose M D Alexander
Contact Rose: alexanderrose185@gmail.com

He Set the Captives Free and *Riverina Girl* are available on digital platforms.

Reference List

John Chapter 4 New Living Translation (NLT)
Loretto Hospital Griffith - www.Griffithre.com
Murrumbidgee Irrigation Area (MIA) www.wikipaedia.org
The Two by Two's - www.wikipedia.org
Tullibigeal Centenary 1917-2017 A collection of history and family stories compiled by Janelle Ireland
Lippes Loop - www.reproductiveaccess.org
Placenta Previa - www.mayoclinic.org
Little Angel - Rose M Alexander
    Open Up Your Heart Album 2007
Osteo Condritis Dissecans - www.mayoclinic.org -
Yuendumu - www.wikapaedia.org
Song for Hannah- t Rose M Alexander 2008
Christian Communicating International (CWCI) www.cwciaustralia.org
He Set the Captives Free - Victor J Sophios-
He Set the Captives Free Album - Rose M Sophios 2004
No-One Will Ever Take Your Love from Me -Rose M Alexander
Open Up Your Heart Album - Rose M Alexander 2007
Life's Highway - Rose M Alexander
Life's Highway- West'n Rose Album 2009
Riverina Girl - Rose M Alexander

Riverina Girl Album 2012
Mum's Funeral Service 31/10/23
Ethel Orr's 80th Birthday 14/09/24
The Village Retirement Village

Scripture References

Psalm 127:3
Proverbs 22:6
Ephesians 6:4
Mark 11:25
Isaiah 41:10
Psalm 37:7
Psalm 9:9
James 1:17
Psalm 34:18
Psalm 31:7
Joel 2:25
John 3:3
2 Corinthians 6:14
1 Corinthians 10:13
Proverbs 17:17
Psalm 121:7-8
John 10: 27-28
Matthew 25:36, 40
Job 13:15

Isaiah 46:10
1 Corinthians 13:7
Psalm 92:1-3
Job 35:10
Psalm 98: 1, 4-6
John 14:1-3
Ephesians 1:5
Psalm 112:1-3
Ephesians 4:16
Exodus 20:12
Proverbs 27:9
Isaiah 40:31
Lamentations 3:22-24
Philippians 4:6-7
1 Thessalonians 5:18
Psalm 100:4
Colossians 2:6
Isaiah 41:10

www.ingramcontent.com/pod-product-compliance
Lightning Source LLC
LaVergne TN
LVHW041625070426
835507LV00008B/457